MESSAGES FROM THE HEART

PART I

**A Message
from the Deacon**

PART II

**Thursdays
with the Deacon**

Deacon Jim Sura

Content and copy editing by Susan Lamour

Cover and interior images by Barbara Sura

Additional cover and interior layout by Susan Lamour

All scripture quotations are from the

New American Bible

ISBN: 1515060888
ISBN-13: 978-151506088

DEDICATED TO:

My wife, Barb, and our children, Michael, David, Sharon, and Susan, and their spouses, Carole, Nancy, Chris, and Didier, who never lost faith in what I could accomplish.

CONTENTS

MESSAGES FROM THE HEART
PART I—A MESSAGE FROM THE DEACON

PART II—THURSDAYS WITH THE DEACON

GOD SPEAKS...I LISTEN

Like a day in May,
Sun bathes the trees, the flowers, and me.
My beautiful mother enfolds me into her arms.
Joseph stands beside us.

Jesus smiles. He loves us three.

Then I went my way and they stayed beside me.
Totally free, I could choose my path,
To do what the world needs to have done,
To bless my God and country.

Like Zacchaeus, I sin gravely.
But our Father speaks to me as he did to Jesus, saying,
"You are my son.
In you I am well pleased."

And they stay beside me
When I struggle with choices.
What are they? What does God wish of me?
What has He told my friends to say to me?

Friends speak. They compliment. What do they say?
With the holy family beside me, they talk to me:
"Leave behind in writing the words God speaks to your
heart, to pass on to the world."

Let this be done! Let the challenge be met!
May God use these words
To help fill the world with love.

Deacon Jim

FOREWORD

I listened to and learned from country western music in my boyhood days, during the late 1930s through the 1950s. Those composers' words said so very much about pure, clean love between men and women, about God, and about loving members of families who lived together, worked together, and ate together with respect in their homes. Country western music spoke to the world about purpose, about respect for every individual, and his/her life's wishes.

Many of us learned and sang those songs! A great deal of my own life's philosophy came through them. One line from those long-ago songs jingles in my mind today and even more so as I advance in years:

> *"It's not what you take with you when you leave this world behind. It's what you leave behind you when you go."*

I was the twelfth of thirteen children born in 1932 to my very committed mother and father, Peter Sura and Mary Kalis Sura. We were farmers who worked the land with horse-drawn machinery and the strength of our own bodies wherever and whenever that was called for.

We raised our food from a variety of large and small farm animals and a large garden. My mother and sisters kept up the garden and house and worked in the field when they were needed. The men worked the fields and took care of the livestock.

Upon turning eighteen, my siblings had to leave home to find their own place in the world. World War II came and went. Two of my brothers were called. In my young years, I watched as my father, and especially my mother, said good-bye to each of two of their sons as they left to be shipped out to the European war zone. I'll never erase those pictures from my mind. It was also then that my deep, admiring feelings for women were born.

Women are strong, but their tender hearts are filled with love. Observing my mother engrained deep, permanent feelings in me that women "should be" set high in a place of honor to be served and treated with tender loving care. I believe a woman would give up her own life for her spouse and any of her children...what love lies in some hearts!

These teen years, indeed, provided experiences that caused me to become the man I have been throughout the rest of my life. It is the time when the actions, feelings, and goals of those we love, as well as those who hurt us, come together to form a person's feelings and personality.

From these formative years, many beautiful friends come to mind, besides family. Among them are religious leaders, teachers, and especially the men on our high school football staff. Still vivid are Coach Frank Studley, Coach Arvid Schmeckpeper, Coach Louis Philippi, and up there "next to God," our head coach, Mr. Harvey Shew.

Why do I hold Mr. Shew up next to God?

First, in four years **not once** did I ever hear a derogatory or four-letter word come from him.

Second, he did all he possibly could to let everyone know any and all the good things each one of us did that helped the team. Every one of us got the highest awards he could give.

One of the most beautiful rewards he gave me was that, through him, everyone in my hometown of Little Falls, Minnesota, knew me, my parents, and siblings. This small boy and his family from our small farm were suddenly loved by ten thousand people, most of whom we didn't know.

Third, every Thursday night as practice ended, Mr. Shew, a non-Catholic, commented that Fr. Edward Rammacher held Mass at 7:00 a.m. on Friday and we could use all the help we could get.

To me, what coach Shew said was on par with the Word of God. This was the beginning of daily mass for me. Additionally, my dear mother had taught me to love God's mother, and I recited the rosary in bed each night. We won most of our games, and I became a sincere believer.

Above all this, my coach helped me enroll in college, where I continued playing and where I expanded more and more into our wonderful world. It was also where my interest led me to a happy, wonderful life in sports and my church.

I hope and pray that my influence as a teacher and coach may have led young people to a happier, healthier spiritual life.

These past sixty-plus years, I thought over and over, *What might the world benefit the most from what I leave behind?*

Yes, I have some ideas.

First, I hope and pray that I leave Barbara, my dear wife, a gift of true love, financial security, and bright and fond memories of our many years together. I hope that she feels unburdened from all the concern and care she gave me in my late and dependent years.

Second, we have given the world four beautiful and warm children who will carry on the works of love and truth that we have practiced.

Third, and very important, with Barb's help and our children's, we have left with each home we have lived in…a garden! A garden that grew nourishment for family and friends and a garden that filled the landscape with beautiful flowers—a place visited by butterflies and birds that gave happiness to so many.

There is one more benefit I hope I can bring. I hope that these *messages from my heart*, contained in the pages of this book, can help make God's world more complete.

The messages compiled first from Part I—*A Message from the Deacon,* consist of weekly bulletin messages to the parishioners of Our Lady of the Snows in Bigfork at a time when the Oblates had left the parish and we became a mission of Grand Rapids.

The second part of my book, Part II—*Thursdays with the Deacon,* consists of homilies on the Gospels of our Lord that I wrote and delivered at weekday masses and occasionally on Sundays during the liturgical year. My warm and wonderful friends of Saint Joseph's Catholic Church and Community in Grand Rapids have encouraged me to have them published.

Acknowledgments
And
Diaconal Journey

My heart and fond thank you go out to all our friends from Our Lady of Snows Parish in Bigfork, Minnesota, and Saint Joseph's in Grand Rapids, Minnesota, for their good will and warm care, encouraging me to write my personal words about the gospels.

My thanks also go out to all the women and men whose help directly led me to make and carry out this mission.

Barbara (Weyrens), my loving wife, encouraged my every effort. She was always ready to put her personal ambitions aside to help me achieve my writing goals, assuming the brunt of the work for the project. I credit her for bringing this dream to fruition.

Our children, Mike, Dave, Sharon, and Susan, along with their spouses, Carole, Nancy, Chris, and Didier have been a blessing from God, and all stand ready to help and support me in all my efforts and in their own unique ways—whether it is helping at the cabin or our home in town, or just to lend a listening ear.

Father Frank Ryan, OMI
Encouraged me to enter into diaconal life

Beyond family, are many friends, especially the priests who were inspirational in Barb's and my church-committed life. Among them, Fr. Frank Ryan, OMI, our pastor at Our Lady of the Snows, encouraged us through the diaconal program, leading to my ordination. He then relinquished some of his own time and duties so I could perform the faculties of my ordination.

Later, Fr. Larry Antus, OMI, became the pastor of OLS. Again, I enjoyed my diaconal duties to the fullest. Fr. Larry (now deceased) was a very caring priest who accepted everyone right where his or her personality was and tenderly helped each individual grow in his or her spiritual life. This is the one-third of every man and woman's life that often fails to develop to a healthy degree. It was during this

Father Larry Antus, OMI
Introduced me to Thistledew's ministry

time that I began accompanying Fr. Larry to Thistledew Correctional Boys Camp in Togo, Minnesota, for weekly mass. After Fr. Larry left OLS, I became the Catholic Chaplain at Thistledew, a duty I held and loved for the next twenty-plus years.

Laying on of Hands
During my Ordination
1983

Deacon Dennis Anderson,
Bishop Robert Brom,
Myself

Time passed, and the Oblates could no longer supply priests to fill our parish needs. They left us, and OLS became a mission of Saint Joseph's in Grand Rapids.

Fr. David Tushar was pastor at Saint Joseph's, thus our pastor at OLS. I was accepted with open arms and asked to do diaconal duties at home in Bigfork and at Grand Rapids. Every month, Father David called on me to do baptisms at his church in Grand Rapids, and monthly homilies at Bigfork. At all Saint Joseph's clergy meetings, I received his invitation to attend. I was treated, by the priests present, as a needed and wanted clergyman.

Baptism

It was at this time that Barb and I (along with my secretary from school, Marcie Lindgren) produced the weekly bulletins at OLS. In each bulletin I composed "A Message from the Deacon." It is these messages that make up the first section of this book.

Fr. Tushar moved on, which is often required in priestly life. Again, I was blessed with a warm pastor, Fr. Tom Radaich, who had me come to Saint Joseph's from Bigfork to preach monthly at weekend masses

Blessing by Bishop Schnurr
To proclaim the Gospel

Two years later, School District #318 granted my retirement. Barb received a transfer to teach in Grand Rapids. We moved there in 1998. Bishop Schweitz immediately transferred me to Saint Joseph's, where Fr. Tom gave me an open invitation to be part of any and all committees. At each meeting he pleasantly introduced me as his "appreciated" deacon. I felt very accepted at my new parish. Saint Joseph's is blessed with an unbelievably huge number of Fr. Tom's created committees. Each, he attended, directed, and evaluated.

I was, again, in a parish that had great respect for ordained clergy, and soon Fr. Tom became aware of my personal strengths and wishes to administer, and he made room for me. Every Tuesday (and later, every Thursday), morning homilies were mine to give And every six weeks I gave the weekend homilies. These in turn became the beginnings of the second half of this book, Part II— Thursdays With The Deacon.

At funerals, I was on the altar with Fr. Tom. Occasionally, I did wakes, funerals, and weddings, when mass was not said.

I worked very closely with a well-run RCIA (Rite of Christian Initiation of Adults) headed by

Witnessing Marriages

my good friend (now deceased), David German. He retired and I inherited the program, having close communication with Fr. Tom.

RCIA—
Right of Christian Initiation of Adults

Fr. Tom was transferred to Duluth and Fr. Jerry Weiss was transferred to Grand Rapids. Shortly after this, Fr. Steve Daigle moved to OLS. Knowing that I loved the people of Bigfork, he invited me to preach there monthly, since I no longer delivered weekend homilies in Grand Rapids. I was again very happy to preach often to my good friends.

At the magic age of seventy-five, clergy are required to submit their resignations. I submitted mine and retirement from the job I loved was upon me. Fr. Jerry, however, knowing how much I enjoyed doing certain ministries, gave me free reign to continue.

For several years I continued with prayer services at Thistledew. I continue to proclaim the Gospel and deliver the homily at Thursday morning liturgies. I also continue to minister to the sick and dying with prayers and Eucharist.

MESSAGES FROM THE HEART

PART I

A MESSAGE FROM THE DEACON

Our Lady of the Snows Church in Bigfork, MN
As it appeared in the early 1960s

Barb Sura, '72

CHAPTER 1

FORGIVENESS

OF

ONESELF AND OTHERS

"We must forgive ourselves before
we can forgive others."

INTRODUCTION TO CHAPTER 1

FORGIVENESS

Thistledew Correctional Facility is a state correctional camp for junior and senior high school boys who are in trouble with the law. The camp is situated in the woods on Thistledew Lake near Togo, Minnesota (about thirty miles north of Bigfork, Minnesota). The boys are sent here by the court system as an alternative to jail, and they go through a very structured program (including schooling) before they graduate from the program and return home.

Bringing the words of Jesus to the boys at Thistledew continued on for some twenty-plus years. The last priest who ministered there was Fr. Larry Antus, OMI (Oblates of Mary Immaculate), while he was pastor at Our Lady of the Snows in Bigfork, some thirty miles from the facility. Whenever Fr. Larry was unable to go, he would have me do a communion service for the Catholic boys.

Our Lady of the Snows became a Mission of Saint Joseph's in Grand Rapids in 1990, and at that time the pastor of Saint Joseph's relinquished the job at Thistledew, and I continued to go there every Friday evening. At the time, it was a contract position with the State of Minnesota, and I was paid as a counselor (which is what I have a master's degree in) and as the Catholic chaplain.

Several years ago, the state finances for the program stopped. The Protestant minister, Pastor David Gabriel of Bigfork, and myself continued going because those teenage boys so looked forward to hearing the stories of Jesus. Catholic boys who wished to go to confession received that sacrament from a priest who would travel with me on those occasions. When the priest did accompany me to administer the sacrament of reconciliation, he would also say Mass so the boy(s) could receive the Eucharist.

Thistledew Ministry

Any of the boys were welcome to attend my prayer service, and they could volunteer to do a reading at the service.

Many are the rewards the boys gave to me. On one occasion, one boy, a tall, pleasant young boy, came to me after prayer. In his hand was a glow-in-the-dark rosary. As the rest gathered around, he told us, "My grandmother gave this to me. She said it will be my salvation, but I don't know what it is."

We talked about Jesus and Jesus' mother.

The following week each boy received a booklet from me on how to say the rosary. Everyone, including the non-Catholics, asked for and received a rosary from me. We sat together after our service and said all the prayers through the first decade.

After that, they asked to recite the entire rosary, and we did so each week. Soon, each boy, Protestants included, with help, led the decades, and eventually, all the rosary prayers. This continued until the group graduated.

These junior and senior high school-age boys were so intent and eager to learn about Jesus, His love, forgiveness, and the peace He brings to our lives, that being with them for that hour each week provided me with the incentive to eagerly drive 120 miles round-trip.

God called me into the diaconate some thirty years ago. He has filled my life with many such warm and beautiful graces.

I am retired now, but my pastor, Fr. Jerry Weiss, gives me free reign on what ministry I wish to do. One of my fondest ministries was when I conducted weekly trips to the boys at Thistledew and experienced the challenge of teaching them forgiveness, especially of themselves.

Thistledew Ministry

"…In his name,
penance for the remission of sin is to be preached to all nations…"
✝

These words of Jesus from Luke 4:47 gave me a jolt and opened a new insight to help break some old habits. They gave me another weapon to fight the sins that had pestered me from early youth. I confessed them, prayed over them, and struggled with them, but they kept popping back, muddying my peace.

Good intentions, contrition, and prayers have effects, but old habits run deep. The magic word in this line is "penance." Imagine the effect if, when temptation occurs, one turns to an act of love or kindness instead of dwelling upon sin. This is penance and it produces purity of soul.

There is more. This act of purity must extend beyond family and friends. Jesus tells us that even the devil does that much. So, how far should one carry this act?

I'm sure that some of you, like me, have had some friends turn their backs when you offer them kindness. They reject any gesture of love. There's the risk of emotional pain, and even anger so severe that more security is found by ignoring their presence.

In these cases, I am sure God will be pleased if, rather than let anger fester in my heart, I dwell upon the good this person has done. This is truly doing penance and it is not easy.

But think about it. By our own sins, we stab the hearts of those who love us far worse than anyone else in our lives.

Repentance helps, but to force oneself to walk a mile in the shoes of one who rasps our patience raw is truly a step into beautification of the soul. It is a tough walk upon a path that is used only by a few, but it is the first step leading to where few have ever gone.

The end is a reward, achieved by very few, and a joy enjoyed by only those few who care to tread that path.

How far I go is between God and me. You try it, too. You will enjoy more happiness than you've ever known.

GOD BLESS.

John's Gospel (17:11) presents a scene with Jesus opening in
prayer with the Father:
"Jesus looked up to heaven and prayed to the Father:
'O Father most holy protect them with your name
which you have given me
that they may be one even as we are one.' "

He enmeshed himself with the Father. I feel awed by His ability, as man, to melt into a single unit with the being of all that is good. Jesus the man, was like us in some ways, but far above us in feeling and giving affection.

Whenever He communicated with God, He shut himself entirely into a space that excluded everything but the two of them. They existed in total with each other. This was singleness of spirit that eliminated all feelings of distance. There existed a totality of divine unity and love.

Because of their oneness, the son knows that His Father will never offend anyone. He knows that the Father has total trust and will never interfere in people's lives unless asked to do so, and then allowed to do so.

He knows God will never make anyone uncomfortable or expect what one is not prepared to give.

In such prayer there is perfect happiness, perfect good will, and a softness and grace in personal perfectness. He provides us here a tiny glimpse into what God is like and how a better prayer life may come to be a fuller graceful experience.

These beautiful words from Jesus show us what to look for and desire from the world and from our friends. They allow us to understand that just as He meshed with the Father, we, too, can grow continually closer into a meshing existence with Him, as well as with the world and all we love.

In existing with Him, we can offer more love; we can make everyone feel that we promote them and don't want to offend them; we don't doubt their abilities, or expect anything from them they do not care to give.

From 1 John 4:13, "Yet if we love one another God dwells in us, and His love is brought to perfection in us!"

Our being boils down to becoming as God-like as possible.

First, we must understand our "self," because *self* is where everything issued from God originates.

Secondly, we need to evaluate what messages we send out, because these are the causes of all that comes back to us a hundredfold.

Thirdly, "God is love." So the more love we experience for self, friends, and the world, the more of God we possess.

So…we should take some quality time each morning before beginning our day to become aware of our feelings toward those we expect to touch that day. Let's ask ourselves, "How does Jesus feel about these people and how would He treat them if He were in my shoes?" Then raise your degrees of love for yourself and go to work. You will be more like Jesus than you were yesterday.

GOD BLESS.

"Be like thoughtful men,
Make the most of present opportunities.
Do not continue in ignorance."
(Ephesians 5:15–17)
✝

Men, women, and children who are open hear Him and pay attention. They tend to the small things, using them in the proper place and at the correct time. This, however, we are not to confuse with trivial thoughts that fail to produce growth.

Jesus says, "Be thinking people. Keep your minds filled with thoughts that lead to the accomplishment of what you put your hand to."

No, we are not to be "sticks in the mud." God wants us to be happy. He wants us to have an occasional "belly laugh," the kind that may continue until tears come and the stomach gets sore. Let it be laughter, though, about wholesome and holy things.

This chapter begins with Saint Paul speaking these words, "As for lewd conduct or lust of any kind, let them not even be mentioned among you. Nor should there be any obscene, silly, or suggestive talk. No fornicator, no unclean or lustful person has any inheritance in heaven."

As you can see here, God didn't leave anything to chance. He is as specific and to the point as anyone can be. Yet He comes through very gently, speaking softly in His divine way. In time, everyone will have heard and, as He promises, come into His fold.

So how can this be summed up in an easy-to-remember, practical thought that we can turn to whenever we drift to the edge of sin? To mess through, doing only "just enough" is mediocrity; it is sloth.

Mediocre, slothful people allow their minds to wallow in thoughts of fornication and lust to find excitement. Such thoughts eventually

---

lead to like actions. Actions of these types force feelings of deep shame, extreme sorrow, and emotional scars to their victims. Being mindful of this is the only way to wholesome pride.

How much more beautiful the world will be when everyone hears and believes, when self-discipline prevails, and we will all feel proud of everything we do. Then, love for all of God's gifts will be the way of life. This is wisdom; it produces health to mind and body.

Until everyone comes into this fold, however, you and I can listen to His gentle voice and enjoy a lifetime of peace...even in the midst of troubles.

GOD BLESS.

The Passion Narrative...

Thirty-three years upon Earth with all its sinful attractions, and He remained pure. He possessed the power of God, yet remained totally humble in complete servitude. He gave everyone what they asked for without reservation.

Jesus never allowed himself to feel used or angry about people's demands. He just gave. After all this, some He had served, because of fear and jealousy, had Him bound and stripped naked, slapped Him, spit into His face, and whipped Him until, from loss of blood, He fell senseless to the ground. Then they nailed Him to the cross where He hung until His head fell from total exhaustion, shut off His breath, and He died of strangulation.

I think that in such a situation, I would, in anger, wish to "even the score." Some of my friends and loved ones would move against such persecutors in revenge, but social chaos would be the result.

This scenario of humankind has been replayed over and over.

Because of fear, and violent nature, humankind needs police forces, armies trained to kill, and weapons capable of annihilating everyone and destroying the world. With these, some achieve the power to strike fear into hearts, subdue opponents, and obtain kingly treatment.

This mode of living is exciting, but it also creates fears and the need for telling half-truths, and thus anxiety. These must seek their needed peace through therapists; some overuse alcohol and tobacco; others muffle their pained minds with narcotics. Society contains many messy minds.

We can name many whose lives were positive toward their brothers and sisters. Their names remain long upon the lips of those who noticed their lifetime was devoted to serving and turning their backs to glory.

While this story of humankind's imperfect lives is continuous, that of Jesus happened only once, but in all its quiet and subtle ways, it is taking possession of the world. It may seem that the attractive, noisy ways of the devil have the upper hand, but the ever-present results of God's promises only add to the beauty of His presence to those who discover Him.

Today calls us, quite loudly, to this discovery. It begins the celebration of His final week as man. The Triduum are days of shame, and death, and pain, but it ends in triumph over death, glory unmatched anywhere, and an everlasting promise. It proves that those who suffer in silence will not only triumph over death, but will also receive a place in eternal glory and never-ending happiness.

My friends, may the life and death of Jesus inspire you to greater heights of godliness so your life here will be filled with shining glory, the warmth of love for everyone, and the full joy of all the beauty of this world. May God's blessings make it so.

GOD BLESS.

The Golden Calf: Exodus 32:7–14
Witnesses to Jesus: John 5:31–47
✞

This chapter happened just an unbelievably short time after the Jews had seen God's powerful love for them in Egypt at the Red Sea, and after they vowed to follow His directions.

They are at Mount Sinai.

Moses has been gone from them for less than four weeks. They have dismissed everything that had happened and returned to idolatry. Of the least expected of the Jews, it was Aaron who collected their gold jewelry, melted it, and formed the gold calf they danced around and prayed to.

God does not appear to be surprised by this, although He did become offended. He called them "stiff necked," meaning that it was almost impossible to change them. He had a simple solution: Let His wrath end their lives and He would start anew with the family of Moses.

Moses, however, convinced Him to refrain. He pointed out that the Egyptians would interpret this to mean that God could not control His people so He destroyed them. Also, it is not even possible for Him to break "His" covenant with their ancestors.

Moses was their intercessor, hinting to us the intercessory power held by our Saints and the Blessed Virgin Mary.

God accepted Moses' argument, so He changed His plan. He is God, who will change His plan when asked to do so and we have faith that He will. Our Saints and Blessed Mother have faith and He listens.

In Barb's and my lifetime both of our strong young sons had accidents most people are not likely to live through. Our deep prayers to God and asking Mary to pray for us resulted in

----

miracles. God spared their lives for us. Today they are men with families and jobs that call for intelligence and great physical strength. Prayers from the heart and faith in God's love brought them home to us.

John's Gospel carried on the story of divine love. God is OK with forgiveness when we turn to Him, confess to our priests, and ask our saints and Mary to intercede. Besides, we have Jesus with us, who makes it His job to bring everyone home to the Father and to eternal happiness.

God's big message comes through here, again, in little hints. The Jews, God's special people, lost trust in Him. Their community was nearly annihilated from the Earth. It was avoided through one man's powerful faith and intercession. We too, you and I, trust in Him to answer our prayers. Also, we have Jesus at our side.

God says, "Ask for miracles, stay faithful, continue loving. I will answer each one."

I feel very strongly today about God's recent gift: He has sent us a Pope whose qualities are much needed by the world. He shows a very deep example of humility and charity. A man/woman who is humble of heart will say, "I am going to use what I have at my disposal for the needy. I ask you to follow me and pray for the most good to happen." Please pray for Him and for yourselves.

GOD BLESS.

Luke 13: 22–30
The Lord forgives through discipline
✝

Is it hard to get into heaven? Jesus seems to say it is when He warns, "Try to get through the narrow door."

Compare this thought with an incident on a busy highway. There is an accident and the police close off all lanes, leaving only a single passage.

Only a narrow passage is like the narrow door. All traffic slows down, even sometimes becoming stop-and-go over long periods of time. People will be bunched up at the narrow door, trying to squeeze through the narrow opening. Sin is like this accident that caused all the trouble.

This image is what it means to get to heaven.

But let's think about it clearly. Actually only one person "has" to get through the door. That person is Jesus. And in the mystery of His death and resurrection, He has passed into heaven. All we have to do is to make sure we stay united to Him. Many bodies do not have to pass through. Only one does: the body of Christ. He is the body of the church.

Jesus did give a second warning: "People will protest to the master, 'we ate and drank in your presence,' but the master will say 'away from me you evil doers, I do not know you.'"

This is disturbing because we eat and drink in Jesus' presence at mass. We partake of His body and blood. Obviously, a mere passive participation in mass is not enough.

Receiving communion without a devotion—a devotion that moves us to allow Jesus to change our lives—is of little spiritual value. What we do at mass, especially in receiving communion, "must" influence the way we live

----

Jesus does not teach in our streets, but He does teach in our church, in the readings and in our priests' homilies. That is why we "must" take to heart the lessons of the scriptures, such as that from the letter to the Hebrews: "My children do not disdain the discipline of the Lord nor lose heart when he reproves you. For whom the Lord loves, he disciplines."

Yet, within it all, the necessary requirement is that we be faithful people and that we remain with Christ "in His body, the church." That is the way to make sure we will make it past all the fuss and bother of this world into the eternal kingdom of heaven.

GOD BLESS.

CHAPTER 2

HUMILITY

TO

GOD'S WISHES

"A humbled heart is a fulfilled heart."

INTRODUCTION TO CHAPTER 2

HUMILITY

The farm was my beginning. Some nonfarm persons looked down upon farm people because we were different.

Life began for me in 1932, in the midst of the great depression. I was at the tail end of a family of fifteen. As soon as my siblings were old enough, they moved out to relieve shortages at home. Being twelfth in the line, I didn't realize that some of the oldest were my brothers and sisters. I loved these people and they loved me... But what a great joy it was to discover after those hard times had passed, that they were my very family!

I was the first member of my family to attend high school. Having been taught to respect—even honor—other people, especially authority, I was well accepted by my peers and my teachers.

One Friday evening in my freshman year, my bus stayed in town to let us watch a football game. I admired the boys on my home team, and I knew I could do a good job of playing, too. I also knew that my father would not approve of me asking others to do my chores at home in order for me play...so I put my wishes on hold.

One day my physical education teacher, Mr. Harvey Shew, told me in class that I showed such deep love for physical activity and I was so physically strong that I should ask permission to try out for football. That was all I needed.

At first Pa totally dismissed my request, but over the winter I kept stating my wishes. Finally I said, very politely, "I'm going out." There was no negative reply.

We had spring football then and there I found a place of freedom where I could release all my energies and pit my strength against opposing forces.

I spent a lot of time at home talking about my times on the football field. My coaches and teammates played one of the most gratifying parts in my life, helping to make it as it is today.

Mr. Shew held the highest ideals of any human being I've ever known and was the most artistic man at passing them on.

Coach
Harvey Shew

Each fall, he drove home one great point: "Boys, if you came out here, today, for your own gain and glory, do yourself and me a favor. Go back into the school building and turn in your gear. There are many people who are making great sacrifices so you can be here. Prepare for and play for their pleasure. "

He further explained, "Your parents, your families are sacrificing for you. Our school is paying for your equipment, for this field. Play for your school. The business people contribute financially toward these ends and they give their time to help out. Thank all these by playing football as excellently as you can. They will be happy and proud of our team. My job is to help you become the best football players you can be. Play as hard as you can…but PLAY CLEAN! If I see anyone playing "dirty" in any way, that person will be sitting here on the bench for the rest of the game."

In my four years as a Little Falls Flyer, I never once heard coach Shew say an off-color word.

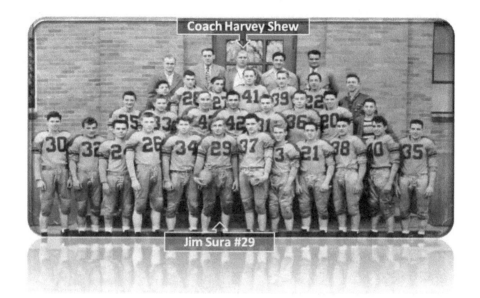

Coach Harvey Shew

Jim Sura #29

To add another reason for my love of football, it became my ticket to get through college and I spent thirty-five years of my life coaching. After thirty-five years as a football coach, I never forgot my days on the field, and all of those memories are super.

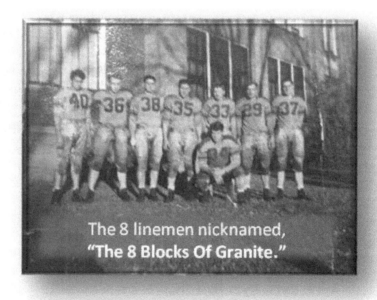

The 8 linemen nicknamed,
"The 8 Blocks Of Granite."

I tried hard to pass on the help God had offered me. Most parents were happy with my coaching methods, but there were doubters.

The spirit in a person's heart is the third person of God. He is with each athlete to whatever degree he allows. When a football team lines up and everyone is filled with the Holy Spirit, all they have been coached to do reaps results far above what they think they are capable of. God fills them with speed and quickness far above what is normal. So a great deal comes to him who turns to the truth—especially when an entire team or group comes to Him.

God has created. Now He uses all of His creation to help us find that built in to us is all the potential we need to accomplish what He sets before us for peace and happiness of all creation. To use our spiritual forces in the right place at the right time brings us to happy heights and fills us with tranquility…Thus, my homilies.

GOD BLESS.

"The reign of our God and the authority of his anointed one are at hand."
✝

God chose to create you and me to have a life on this Earth, and He gave us His divine love and promise, if we seek it, of peace and joy. The world we live in offers beauty, but also sorrow. Because of our strengths, we find His joy and peace.

The stronger we grow, the more effective we become as His hands, His feet, and His lips. For this reason He so carefully brought together all the marriages from the beginning of man up until He formed you and me. Each of our ancestors gave us something from himself or herself making us unique and providing us strength and knowledge enough to withstand the temptations and pains coming from outside. He himself is present for us at times when we cannot control that which may become overwhelming. He also gave us one another for this purpose.

If ever you should have doubt, turn to the Bible. Today's excerpt from the book of Revelation showed us the importance of each individual. (I say showed-past tense-because these words were said many years prior to the time of Christ on Earth.)

It speaks of the Virgin Mother from among the twelve tribes of the Jews. She wails in pain as she gives birth to the baby who will create the Christian community and the sacraments through which man, for the rest of the history of the world, will receive the directions and the graces to carry out the will of the father.

It also tells of the very powerful, determined devil who was waiting at the foot of Mary to destroy this baby the moment He became a living reality. The unlimited power of God, however, destroyed the efforts of Satan. God, we see here, always prevails. His will shall never end. It shall continue until the end of earthly time.

The closing lines from this excerpt sum this up:

"Then I heard a loud voice in heaven say,
'Now have the salvation and the power come.
The reign of our God and the authority of His anointed one
are at hand.'"

Here we are told that we are living in the final phase of His divine plan. There will be no more total destruction through natural disasters, or another Messiah. All this has been accomplished. We have been given everything we need and our hands are to accomplish His purpose.

Through Saint Paul's letter today, we hear of the importance of man doing God's will with His graces to overcome the devil and carry out God's plan.

Look. Listen. Grow. What you accomplish can only be done by you. Do the best you can.

GOD BLESS.

"There is no need for them to disperse.
Give them something to eat yourselves."
✝

Now that God has created the world, the plants, the animals, and humans, He devotes a lot of time helping us through our freedom of choices to learn why we have been blessed with a life on Earth.

Early in the life of humankind He spoke through prophets. Some listened, but many didn't and lived for worldly pleasures. As people drifted into corrupt living, many natural disasters occurred that entirely destroyed the world and most of the people. For millions of years this happened. It continues even now and will until the end of time.

Today's gospel story does a terrific job of explaining it all. Saint Matthew describes for us a picture of Christ's actions, which in the course of one day, plays out the entire drama of what being a living man or woman is all about. As we listen to it, one can visualize the story as the scenario of a good play upon a stage.

It starts with a thirty-year-old man. He has just received word that the cousin whom He loved greatly has been killed. He gets into His boat and rows to the shores of a very quiet place where He can mourn and pray for Saint John.

However, as He climbs out of the boat, He sees before Him a great multitude of people (more than ten thousand of them). Since He has not yet begun His public life, we will assume that these are people who have learned to love Him through His work as a carpenter.

As He looked out upon them, He knew they were there to help Him through His sorrows. He was deeply moved with pity because of the hardships they had endured to come to Him. There were many sick among them, and in His great love, He moved among them, thanking them and curing those who were sick.

When the day ended, His disciples came to Him, advising that He send the crowd home or to wherever they could buy supper. The implications here lead us to believe that many of them had gone without food and water that entire day. His reply was a foretelling of their jobs as disciples, as well as what our jobs are to be:

"There is no need for them to disperse.
Give them something to eat yourselves."

The drama continued. He instructed the people to sit down on the grass. He blessed the five loaves and the two fish, broke the bread, and then: "...gave the fish to the disciples who in turn gave them to the people."

Matthew's account of the story tells us that, "everyone who ate the food Jesus blessed were filled and satisfied."

We are not shown the ending because the play isn't over. We know that in order to find true satisfaction, we must eat the bread Jesus gives us through the hands of His disciples.

We also know that whenever disaster strikes, our hands must become the hands of Jesus to feed the unfortunate, and in our day this is being done. Many contribute food and money to our food shelves, to our starving brothers and sisters in Africa, and in our inner cities.

We see many good people leaving the comforts of home to aid those in flooded areas, building sandbag embankments against destructive waters. Others send drinking water to those places. We have many young people, each summer, going into the inner cities to help build houses for the homeless.

Yes, drama is still going on, and you and I are the actors.

Our world continues to go out to those disaster strikes and all the less fortunate.

If, however, we as a people should decide to just sit back and live for ourselves without bothering over those whose lives are being ruined, we will get to watch our world completely fall under the destructive hands of men and women who look for their fill among riches and power.

Continue your works of charity and love. Yours are the saving hands that carry out God's will.

GOD BLESS.

"Be holy, for I, the Lord, your God, am holy."
Leviticus 19: 2b
✟

In His messages the last two weeks, God has been cautioning us to become conscious of any tendencies toward habitual sin. There is an urgent call to recognize bad habits, and then to avoid the occasions where we may fall into them.

When I was a teenager studying the effects of substances upon the human body, a point was made that still stands out in my mind, though I don't follow it 100 percent of the time. That point was that using alcohol is not harmful to the system if used as God would like us to. Not all users become alcoholics. However, no one knows how alcohol will affect him/her and some will become addicted. The only way to really avoid this unfortunate condition is never to take your first drink.

This is what our holy writers are telling us about sin. Even though our small sins are not really "hell bent" offenses, for some sinners, they are the beginnings of a downhill slide into self-deterioration.

We can avoid chaos if we don't give in to temptations to small sin. The murderer would never have committed that crime if he had not nursed his initial anger.

May you take a few minutes each day to pray or just sit and be quiet and meditate on where you've come from, where you are, and where you want to go. God's promised peace is at hand.

GOD BLESS.

---

*"Give to Caesar what is Caesar's.
But give to God what is God's."*
-Matthew 22:21
✞

Adults with true conviction and who are productive have grown up
in an environment of honesty and healthy pride.

For them all events are genuine and give meaning to life. They
meet the world's elements whatever they are. They see the good
that is present, correct the wrongs, and try to assess those things
they have no control over. Their families and friends have been
good models. Their homes (the first and most influential school)
have taught them to look for and find beauty in everything and
everyone they encounter. In all, these people have developed
nearly completely.

Along with their growth and the social and economics of society,
they have developed the often-neglected spiritual element. They
have become the souls of our society.

These are the much needed whose influence keeps the seekers
of power and wealth from destroying all. These are the needed for
the moment and for neglected future generations as our media
continues to downplay the spiritual and glamorize sex and
violence.

In my lifetime, many have recently witnessed the downfall of a
great nation that persecuted religion while it promoted rule by
force. As the Blessed Mother promised at Lourdes, the Soviet
Union did collapse because of our many prayers, and it did not
conquer the whole world, which was its goal. Rebuilding, however,
has gone nowhere.

Pope John Paul II warned that it wouldn't if the leaders neglected
God. His words were, "If you only replace one economic system
with another, it will not work. You must give your country a soul."

Now, after years of political fighting, their economy has hit rock bottom and nothing wholesome has happened politically. President Yeltsin has invited church ministers into the organization of their new government. If these people bring God into the movement, we will, in our lifetime, see a new Russia become a powerful nation once again. No human and no nation can exist in peace without a clean soul.

Today, Isaiah speaks God's words that tell us how worthless man's efforts are when we try to function outside of Him.

"Thus says the Lord to his anointed, 'Cyrus whose Right hand I grasp, subdividing nations before him, And making kings run in his service for the sake of Jacob, my servant of Israel, my chosen one. I am the Lord_and there is no other. It is I who arm you.'"

(Isaiah 45:1, 4–6)

God created everything and only His plan will come to completion.

Our own great country has become a world power and will remain so as long as we continue to govern according to the words of our founders, "One nation, under God, with liberty and justice for all."

This soul, my friends, is you. The fact that you choose to worship God opens you to the peace that He promised. Make it a major element in your life. What you do today leaves lasting results upon the world of tomorrow.

GOD BLESS.

"Take time to look inside yourself.
Clean up as many small faults as you need to."
✝

Amos, the prophet, was killed like other prophets before him, after he pointed out God.

He pointed to some specific ways that the fortunate were abusing the poor, such as cheating on the scales, holding back their produce to get higher prices while the poor starved, and selling the poor the residue from the meat and grain that should have been thrown away.

This was happening many thousands of years ago at the beginning of human relationships. These practices caused the poor to have to sell themselves and their families into slavery.

God says, "I will never overlook these abominations." In other words, sins must be purged somewhere, sometime.

Most of us are not guilty of such horrible practices. However, Amos is telling us that we should take a deep look inside. We may find we are guilty of some lesser degrees of cheating and our consciences have been accustomed to doing these things. Keep in mind that small things are easy to handle, but they need to be handled before they get big.

What we do makes a big impact upon the world. Before we can ask our children to follow God's outlines for happiness, we must first clean up our own faults (pull the plank from our own eye). What we show our children will pass on until the end of time and this makes a big difference to the world.

Because Abraham was an honest, God-loving man, God informed him that he would have descendants as numerous as the stars of the sky and be the father of many nations. He and Sarah had only one child, but in time, this promise happened.

The same promise is made to you and me, and we must never forget that nations have collapsed when they turned away from God and they lost their soul. New nations grow under God and flourish. New nations will be made up of God-loving people.

Take time to look deep inside, and clean up as many small faults as you can. Remember that the good you do will remain long after you are gone.

GOD BLESS.

CHAPTER 3

LOVE

"May your love produce light."

INTRODUCTION TO CHAPTER 3

LOVE

Life is a beautiful gift! Love is our core. It is what we are all about. Love is God and we are created just a little less than God.

Here is a quote from Charles Swindoll's, *Giving Rouge* pg. 209: "What happens to me is 10% of it all. 90% of it all is how I react to it."

How I choose to handle things that happen is what I give to the world. The world grows stronger or becomes weaker as a result of the way I feel and react to its offerings.

The small, seemingly insignificant things I feel and do have a far greater impact upon the world, close at hand and far distant. Many "tiny" things together become "big" things and go out to others as our gifts. They spread and grow and return to us far greater than when they left. They become a part of the lives of many. They are part of my life and they move on into the entire maze of the offerings of all the others in the community, state, country, and world.

My part of all that happens requires — **demands** — that I *listen* to others and to His stories in the Bible, and meditate on His subtle voice.

The following are messages He has spoken through me in my meditations. I offer them with love.

"What would the world be like if
everyone knew the Ten Commandments..."
✟

Today the media gives us many stories of humans' inhumanity to humans. The reports are true, and yes, serious crimes, along with greater degrees of hideousness, are increasing, and they are occurring closer and closer to home—our homes. Why?

Presently, the future is more uncertain than it used to be, and people are confused about the present. For this, men get out their guns and kill to gain luxuries they feel they need to be happy or to "get even" with a person who told them their job has expired.

Jesus says, "Everybody who 'grows angry' with his brother will be liable to judgment; anyone who looks lustfully at a woman has already become guilty of adultery; what I tell you is not to even swear at all." Three of the Ten Commandments, if obeyed, would eliminate the ugliest crimes.

Saint Paul describes the human body as God's temple. The men and women who look inside themselves find a beautiful spirit and discover an abundance of laughter and love. They also find a world filled with peace and plenty and warmth.

What would our world be like if everyone knew the Ten Commandments and lived according to their intent? As honest human beings, though, we have the right to control only one person. That one person, however, sometimes falls into sin, even though he or she is strongly self-disciplined.

The message calls further for spiritual exercise. All of us gain some nourishment and growth through the Sunday Mass experience. Reaching maturity requires a lifetime of these exercises. The strength builder of the spirit is prayer, which happens in many forms. Like any construction, it must be done well, with love and self-sacrifice.

Some look at spiritual development as something that interferes with their progress toward success in the material world. These must be reminded that to let the spirit lie dormant is a failure to develop a major part of humanness. Development of this character adds as much pleasure and richness as physical, mental, and financial growth. It is needed to form a complete human.

Each day may you find new love. May your love produce more light. May we all move toward your light and may all our lights illuminate the world. A person who moves forward into what lies before him or her is a glorious light in a trying world.

GOD BLESS.

Matthew 23: 1–12
Jesus denounces the Scribes and Pharisees
✝

Matthew 23:1–12 presents a picture of Jesus in the midst of a crowd that includes His chosen twelve disciples.

His words are bold, but the message must be told. All who follow the Christian faith need to hear it said, and He, without fear or hesitation, proclaims it, though He knows He will be misunderstood, tortured, and killed for doing so.

"The Scribes and Pharisees have succeeded Moses as teachers; therefore do everything and observe everything they tell you. But do not follow their example. Their words are bold but their deeds are few. They bind up heavy loads, hard to carry, to lay on other men's shoulders, while they themselves will not lift a finger to lighten them." (Matthew 23:1–4)

Jesus goes on to discuss other practices of these teachers of God that we as caring and doing people are to avoid because they do not achieve what being Christian is about. He points to their wearing gaudy clothes that sets them apart, and their habit of taking the places of honor at gatherings.

Now here is where you and I must take care, because if we dwell upon the wrong part of this message, we will fall into the very trap He is warning us against.

We must look less but *listen* deeply. On the surface, it seems like the Lord is condemning these men for their actions. He is not doing this because that would only be gossip and not gospel. He does not condemn or gossip.

Think for a moment about what God has given you. Among all these gifts is that of total free will and a unique personality. The great achievers among us are those who intently "listen" and then move in the direction that wisdom takes them. Each person, being unique, was created to interpret and then perform individually according to his or her own talents.

To look at actions only and accept or reject these leaves one shallow and makes him or her a follower. And followers don't produce much. They repeat the words "me too," spin their wheels, and go only short distances.

Those who intently "listen," who chew and digest what they hear, will visualize how these newly obtained insights fit into their own ways, their abilities, their likes and dislikes, and use them in their own lives. These are the movers. They grow and with them the world grows. They are genuine, active elements in nature. They become one with it and become filled with peace even when the world sometimes seems against them. These are the people whose names never die. They are the famed leaders, and many, like Jesus, live on forever.

My dear friends, God loves you. Love Him back. It only requires a little self-discipline. Spend less time dwelling upon what others are doing. Listen deeply to what they are saying. Be aware to what their words are really implying. Read the words of the Bible. Meditate upon the words of prayer, especially those of the Mass and from the lips of your priest. From all of this, apply it to what you are good at doing. You will grow then. Your life will be filled with peace. You will become a respected leader. The world and everything that's in it will become yours, and you, like Jesus, will ascend to heaven and bring many with you.

GOD BLESS.

"This is my beloved Son…"

✞

The sky opened, a brilliant light enveloped Him, a white dove descended upon Him, and a voice announced, "This is my beloved son. I am pleased with Him. Listen to Him." You and I weren't there, but the men of God chose to write the story, leaving us a vivid picture of this miracle.

Jesus left a rich legacy for our enjoyment. What do we do with it? In every celebration of the Mass we receive small but vivid bits. Do you listen? Some do and even seek more.

Some go to the Bible, read passages, and dwell on their meanings. That is all that is needed. These people develop a deeper knowledge of God and a richer life. The beauty and the luxury of the world is still theirs to enjoy, but they add new dimensions to their lives.

We receive limitless blessings from God and he wants us to use and enjoy every one. He gives us many blessings unless we abuse them. Each has a proper time, place, and purpose. To use any out of its pattern results in sin, eventually sorrow, and even possible destruction of life and property.

Through the common sense way of life, we enjoy to the utmost what God has given us, if we take time to learn who He is and give Him a place among the luxuries.

Life can be constant excitement and joyful expectations if we use all things in their proper places.

To leave God out offsets the natural balance of the order and chaos begins to creep in, harmony slips away, life loses its charm, and we begin to experience uneasiness and even bitterness.

Ask for God's help, and then be open to it! This week when negativism begins to show its ugly head, take a minute to look at

---

your life. Somewhere you lost a blessing; somewhere else you neglected one. Put these back in perspective and life will flow beautifully. Only you, with God's help and rich heritage, can control your feelings and your destiny. No one else can, unless you allow him or her.

GOD BLESS.

John saw the Spirit descend like a dove from the sky…

✝

Listen to the words of Saint John the Baptist: "The one who sent me to baptize said: 'When you see the Spirit descend and rest on someone, it is He! He will baptize with the Holy Spirit.' John saw the Spirit descend like a dove from the sky. This is God's chosen one."

How powerful! When God moves in one's life and he or she opens to it, there is nothing that comes near this experience in the magnitude of joy and spectacular greatness.

To comprehend this, just dwell a moment upon the twelve apostles, the men who walked with Him and really knew Him. They very happily accepted persecution and death because of the love they felt. Will you and I ever become so familiar, so fond, that our love will reach this level?

Isaiah opens our eyes with these words God communicated to him, "The Lord said to me: 'You are my servant, my Israel, through whom I show my glory. I will make you a light to the nations; that my salvation may reach to the ends of the earth.'"

Consider this, my friends! You and I are God's chosen. These words force us to stop and think upon who we really are. With these words, God has called you and me to lead others to heaven.

How frightening! We have seen the response to this from others. The blessed virgin asked, "How will this happen?" but then replied, "Be it done unto me according to thy word." *(Luke 1:37-38)*

My friends, these words reach out to everyone in His chosen community. Dwell then, for a moment, on how important you are. What is your answer? God loves you very much. You are vital to the salvation of many.

GOD BLESS.

...Jesus was met by a Leper who came for a cure...

✝

According to Jewish law, which Jesus spoke to Moses and Aaron, lepers had to isolate themselves from everyone and warn those who came near that they were "unclean." This information as far as knowledge goes, is quite trivial...or is it?

To help us understand love and other human drives, outstanding speakers and writers very carefully give us symbols. Symbolizing is using very familiar objects to represent those things we cannot see or feel because they do not have mass or are not physical objects. Human feelings are nonphysical elements; we know they exist, but they are not physical objects.

This is what I see our great writers today doing with leprosy. Jesus came to a city to teach. He was immediately met by a leper who begged for cure. Jesus granted his wish. He commanded the leper not to tell anyone, but to go tell his priests so they could grow in faith and enthusiasm.

This very happily renewed man heard very little of what Jesus said. He was so filled with joy over his worldly gift he didn't even go to the priests with the words Jesus had instructed him to carry there. Instead, he went about disobeying the Lord's command by telling everyone about his miraculous cure.

This cured man, through his disobedience, made it difficult for the Lord to go among the crowds to teach as He deeply longed to do. This man, like the many others Jesus cured, told only the story of receiving his greatest wish. As a result, the people sought Him to raise Him to an office of honor. Jesus, like all true Christians, wanted no part of this. His job is the same as ours, which is to make known the love the father has and to make ourselves less among others. This is purity.

This lifestyle plants the seeds of divine love more deeply than anything we say because, as we see today, not many listen and hear with any depth. It becomes, then, very important, if we wish to tell the story of the Spirit, that we become doers and givers like Jesus was and is.

My experience, like yours, has been that those who remain uppermost in my mind and heart are the men, women, and children in my life who helped me gain what I wanted most. I'll never forget these people, and I also recall them whenever life becomes difficult and I need to make a difficult decision. Likewise, the actions and the morals of these people have left their impression upon how I feel and act toward the rest of society.

From now on, when you hear or recall the stories from the Bible, if you open wide your mind and heart, the word of God takes deep root and Jesus becomes one of those people you never forget and to whom you turn when your problems become too heavy.

Carry this action one step further. You, yourself, through what you give become the person who comes to mind when someone needs a symbol to turn to when life's cross grows heavy.

In the process, may you make yourself "self"-less. You will become the symbol of who Jesus is.

GOD BLESS.

...the poor, the downtrodden, the dependent, need your love...
✝

God gives us the ability and the sense to see the poor, the downtrodden, the dependent, and those most unjustly and painfully misused by society. We see the neglected widows, orphans, and others who cry for mercy. Saint Paul tells Timothy about his imprisonment and his day in court with all his friends abandoning him, and his knowledge that within a few days, he will be traded shamefully in public and killed. This seems like underdogs are abandoned by God!

To understand, look closely at the importance of *this* very moment in life. The reality is that *this very moment* is all that exists for us. A second ago is past, the next has not arrived. All that exists is right now. What is important about this is the only moment of our lives we need to control and can control is *this very moment,* and my friends, even though we cannot control what someone else is doing to us, we *can* control what *we* do with what is occurring.

We can take pain or sorrow and dwell upon it, become fearful of it, hate it, and let it take over our lives and become negative. The result will be that we will either deny the existence of this reality or we will feel helpless and thus inferior to the world and to those who seem to have their lives under control. Or we will resort to some degree of anger and even become destructive. Some people eventually resort to the most hideous of crimes.

This doesn't have to be. Sirach, Paul, and the writers of Revelations tell us there is another way—a positive way that will turn the world to God and bring the promised peace.

We are told in Sirach, Chapter 35: "The prayer of the lowly pierced the clouds; it does not rest until it reaches its goal, nor will it withdraw till the most high responds, judges justly, and affirms the right." Paul says, "The Lord will bring me safe to his heaven." *(2 Timothy 4:18)*

These men are describing the virtue of hope. We are told here to take each single moment, be it a moment of joy or of deep pain, and really "know" that it is passing, accept it just as it is, and live with it. God is aware of it, too. He loves you above all else, and he will, at the right time, make everything correct. Then we will get through the worst of sorrows, even those we don't think we can handle.

We have been given the gift to see great prophets so we can witness, from their lives, the possibility of living out painful trials, becoming stronger from them, and being, like them, vessels of harmony and love.

May you, like the humble tax collectors, turn to God with your pains. The rewards are beyond human understanding.

GOD BLESS.

"...those who survive have made their robes white
in the blood of Jesus..."
✝

"Those who have survived the great period of trials have made their robes white in the blood of the lamb." *(Revelations 7:14)*

"We shall be like him for we shall see him as he really is." (*1 John 3:2)*

These lines are taken from the two readings today, and along with Matthew's Gospel on the Beatitudes, when lived out, are for us, relief from anxiety and pain and far exceeds prescribed medicine. These lines are our pathway to lives of peace. Jesus and his disciples have told this story in so many different ways, yet many of us have never really heard the message.

In our rapidly changing world, we borrow so much from the past and apply new ideas to them.

Our news media digs into all corners of the lives of man and show us mostly the shameful and sinful. As a result, we get a very distorted picture of true human life. It seems, at times, as though the selfish, the glory seekers, materialists, and those who deny the presence of God rule us.

The truth is, yes, there are far too many such people, and inside each of us exists the potential to follow their practices, and sometimes we do lean that way. The fact is also that these practices and thoughts lead only to feelings of gloom. Gloom leads to darkness. We need light! It is through the teachings and examples of Jesus and the apostles that we find light.

How often in your life have you seen people come face to face with pain and tragedy and respond by going to pieces in anger then either running from reality or seeking revenge?

How often, on the other hand, have you seen friends suffer tragic loss then turn to God and loved ones, work peacefully through it, and come out with love filling their hearts, peace filling their souls, and making life sweeter for all? These have their lives rooted in sainthood. They are the vessels of proof that God is real and that the beatitudes are true.

May God become more real for you each day. Seek Him, listen to Him. He will give your heart a stronger beat and your face a brighter smile. This He promises.

GOD BLESS.

...Turn to God and his people with love...
✝

It seems obvious, though sad, that so many people avoid thoughts about the existence of hell. Perhaps in our search for peace and love, it is too discomforting to recall negatives and pain, but the reality of its presence must be acknowledged.

In our opportunity to live, if we think about our experiences and opposing forces, we see a greater picture. We have saints and merciless criminals; there are celibates and married people, and there are sexual abusers who take all they can get.

We have people who forgive and work for peace and solutions, and we have some who flounder in anger and strive for revenge. Nature gives us terrible storms. She also presents beautiful sunny days. These thoughts crossed my mind after today's readings.

History tells of some weak kings, about some very selfish ones. They were kings under whose rule life was miserable. Then God sent kings like David, "the singer," as he is often called, who ruled with great justice, power, and love, and who had a very devout love and respect for God.

King David was the origin of much in the book of Psalms. Though the descendants of many good kings were weak and ineffective, the main descendant of King David was Jesus, the ultimate of all that is beautiful, good, and strong. He had, and still has, dominion over the whole world, both material and spiritual.

Jesus never worried about food, clothes, shelter, or popularity. He taught, healed, forgave, loved, and lived for the Father with His whole heart and soul. His most beautiful acts happened while He hung, nailed to the cross.

He tolerated the taunts of the people who forgot about the existence of hell.

To the robber who asked his forgiveness, Jesus quietly assured him that he would live eternally in heaven. And among His last words were, "Father forgive them. They do not know what they are doing." *(Luke 23:24)*

May today's stories serve to remind you that no sin is too grievous for divine forgiveness if we give it up and turn to God.

GOD BLESS.

Romans 6: 19–23, Luke 12: 49–53

✝

Jesus wants to set the world on fire about the love the Father has for us all.

That's not an easy job! He also says that those who follow Him must be prepared to make some tough decisions because strong commitment to a cause will bring about division among people. We also name His will to set the world on fire His passion.

The old French connotation of passion is adding strength to feeling. We sometimes speak of romantic attraction and anger as passionate feelings.

A strong drive of passion is the requirement for achieving above and beyond what is normal. It is what drives athletes to peak performances, teachers to inspire students to love learning, and Christian leaders to excite people to listen and learn and to love God who has created our happiness. Passion for the wholesome leads us to eternal life. It leads to success, creates deeper commitment, strength against temptation, and lights a fire in others around us.

Passion for good varies. It is based upon dreams and talents. Holy dreams and actions make us part of the Body of Christ. Our being on fire builds God's "kingdom on Earth."

One whose passion may be to fill his or her own bucket is OK as long as she or he doesn't deplete the elements of the environment. But Jesus implies far more in His words. He tells us to light a flame in everything in life that we put our hands to and to add to all the world. Light a spark of love wherever you go, to whatever you do, and it will grow into larger flames everywhere. These tiny fires perfect us to be highly effective with everything we leave behind and draws out the best along the way. It elicits warmer love from others God sends.

Christ was deeply loved. He was also hated by the men He upset by telling the story of God as a loving God, forgiving, and very generous. Thus, we are to prepare ourselves for some antagonism. Those who do nothing and do that poorly are really not noticed and not highly loved or disliked. Whatever you do, feeling excited about it and doing it for others to enjoy fills the world with greater perfection. Like Jesus, light the world on fire and the will of God becomes more perfected here on Earth because of you!

GOD BLESS.

CHAPTER 4

PEACE

"My peace I give to you…

…It is freely given, but can be lost."

INTRODUCTION TO CHAPTER 4

PEACE

Wherever we turn in society we encounter some loud, boisterous people, and those who seek pleasure in calling attention to themselves and purchasing what money can buy but always falling a bit short of contentment. The new personal attention they gain fulfills them for a short time and then something new must come into place for pleasure to come again.

Life at these levels lacks stability. When all of God's creation keeps its place in the natural order, the world functions smoothly. When an occurrence moves out of its natural way, chaos happens and then all else suffers until the disorder gets corrected.

People are made in God's image. God is love! Thus, people are made of love. Love exists only when we give. Many confuse love as a good feeling. In a way, this is true, but genuine love becomes a good feeling not when we treat ourselves, but when we reach out to make another happy.

When joy is given, happiness and love return to the giver. When humans give love, nature is in harmony. God's will causes all movement to harmonize. Unless we are happy with whom we are, we are not happy with what we have!

Peace in life is our reward when everyone keeps his or her life in smoothness with all else. Our breaking the flow is called sin. We must all know that our sins disrupt life, our sacred gift from God that calls us to peace. Any personal sin breaks the natural flow.

Fornication destroys marriage. Marriage binds and cannot ever be broken because a husband and wife vow to "give" themselves to and for the happiness, welfare, and completeness of the other. Through a lifetime of giving they become "one"—a single unit. If they are not capable of giving, chaos occurs, along with much hurting. This really never heals and so marriage, which is forever until the end of life, is never fulfilling.

The gift of marital love oftentimes becomes an uncontrolled obsession. Misuse here becomes self-gratification and breaks the natural order that was intended, which is to bring happiness to your spouse. Misuse is a sin, and sin hurts everyone. God's gift is intended for married couples to bring peace and joy to others. Marital sins have led to artificial means to fulfillment and to killing babies in the most secure place in the world, the mother's womb. All of this is unnatural and makes marriage unnatural and other people suffer. This will continue to hurt us until all those sins are corrected.

Correcting will only happen when everyone knows and believes the Bible's stories such as Sodom and Gomorra, the Great Flood, and the fall of God's chosen people when they turned away and broke their promise to Him. Happiness and peace return when people return to being givers.

GOD BLESS.

The meek will inherit the earth… (Matthew 5:5)

✞

The prophet, Zephaniah, lived 640 years before Christ. His cry was to avoid false pride and to resist the ways that were popular with the world. It was popular to worship the sun, the moon, the stars, and other idols. It was popular to show off one's success, one's achievements, and high social position. And it was popular to indulge in self-fulfillment and ignore the guides given by God that are the only way to peace and harmony.

He warned that at the Lord's coming the vain will be shamed and cast from their high places, while the lowly will live on in their humility, harmony, and peace.

Saint Paul calls us to grow in knowledge of Christ because only in this wisdom does peace thrive. The more we know Jesus, the more we want to avoid worldly ways and popularity, and the more we make our lives flow within those guidelines of the natural world of all living things.

Since the beginning of humankind, God has had prophets and priests telling us, over and over, the stories about the beautiful effects of the touch of His holy hands. We have seen, over and over, how nations thrived, grew, and became powerful under leaders who ruled according to the Ten Commandments. We have also seen, over and over, what happened when the leaders became corrupt.

As the powerful lead, so do they follow. History shows that the poor pay the initial price of corruption. The powerful place ever-greater demands on them, and eventually find life unbearable. The downtrodden have always had to struggle to gain back a decent place in life. Unfortunately, some turn to violence, and some to mind-altering drugs and alcohol. These have lost God and His promise of peace.

They have been unfortunate. They met false prophets using false promises in the name of God and became enslaved.

Fortunately, a few humble have always remained. These never strayed from the guidelines. They suffered in silence, ever turning their misfortunes over to Him, always extending their hands to the needy, always asking forgiveness for their sins, and living through life with peace in their souls, prayers on their lips, and love in their hearts.

Life holds a certain sweetness for the humble. Wise men and women open themselves to God. They hear His gentle promises, and be they wealthy or poor, their lives are filled with beauty and peace.

God bless you. Take time to read Zephaniah's words. Also, reread the Beatitudes, which Jesus taught six hundred years later. His message never changes. Those who make them the model for their lives, more and more, receive the world in their hands to rule it. This is the heritage to the meek and the humble.

GOD BLESS.

2 Corinthians 13:11:
"Mend your ways. Live in harmony and peace.
Then the God of love and peace will be with you."
✝

Exodus 34 says: "In a cloud, the Lord stood with him (Moses) and proclaimed His name, 'Lord.' Thus the Lord passed before him and cried out 'the Lord, the Lord, merciful and gracious God, slow to anger and rich in kindness and fidelity.'"

During the times we are saddled with pain (physical, mental, and emotional), it seems unlikely that God has much mercy and love for us. This is a genuine human reaction.

I, like many of you, live in constant rheumatic aches. I pray and expect the future to bring relief. Sometimes we suffer the pains of injustice. Some of you have suffered the worst of all, the death of your son or daughter.

Why does God heal some people, but not others? The Bible contains many examples of miraculous healings.

We've heard of the healings at miracle shrines such as Lourdes, Fatima, Sainte-Anne-de-Beaupre at Quebec City, Saint Joseph's Oratory in Montreal, and others. Crutches, wheelchairs, leg braces, remain behind as witness to these healings.

The June 1993 issue of *The Catholic Digest* has an article titled "Healing has many faces," condensed from *The New Covenant* written by Stephen Sheridan. It says, "God always heals. It is just that, many times, it does not happen the way we want it. The criterion of Jesus is this: Will this help you get to heaven?"

In our lives, we experience many wounding problems of various degrees. They range from upsetting words to severed relationships. Some fill us with anger or even hatred. All of these can be cured, but we, ourselves, must take the steps to cure them. Most can be overcome by the passing of time. Some require help from other people (usually a friend, sometimes a professional, usually through confession).

Sometimes healing doesn't happen because (we) fail to forgive. Bitterness replaces love and joy.

Relief sometimes comes through prayer. For us who have experienced it, peace always comes through a *good* confession.

God is genuinely concerned with our well being, but not always on our terms. We know we can depend on Him, though we must first look at what we ourselves are doing to ease the pain. When we look, we have to learn to love what we see. There is help through caring friends, sometimes groups such as AA, NA, Tough Love, etc. God's healing hand works within them.

God wants to heal. He has many means, but (we) must seek to use them. Do not look for miraculous events. Use what He has provided: friends, groups, sacraments, and grace. Turn to each of them. His grace is the final balm.

God bless you. May you learn to live with the selfishness from around you. May you love and forgive. May you find healing where it is, in the numerous forms within the holy hands of God. And that is peace.

GOD BLESS.

God's voice gently calls, giving tenderness and love...
✝

Our media informs us about the many crimes in society. It is correct in doing so because at least we know what needs to be changed to make our world safe.

An English statesman commented that the Europeans look down on America because of our many crimes. So what is the answer? Our leaders need help to find it. It will slow down, somewhat, as we pass tighter gun laws and hire more people—with guns—to hunt down the offenders. Some will get killed; some will be jailed; some will escape; and the types of crimes will change.

Our Bible and history books show that man has never been different. Many search constantly for comfort, wealth, power, and instant pleasure. Envy and jealousy have always led man to plunder, torture, and to hate.

Our religious writers tell us also that man has always been subjected to God's voice gently calling to give us tenderness and love. The quiet majority hears His call and responds. But such feats seldom reach the attention of the world, even though it touches the masses and does overcome evil.

Today's readings bear this out. From one of them, we hear from a very hideous killer from early Christian years. He was a Roman soldier, very effective at finding Christians and torturing them to death. He was highly efficient in wiping out the church and the name of Jesus from his followers. He took great pride in this highly successful venture and was much admired in the Roman social circles. He was also dreaded by the lowly, especially those who found peace in the promises of Christ.

He, though, became very fortunate. In spite of his hatred for Christians, he was greatly loved by a very devout one. He was loved so much by this Christian that he received one of the

---

greatest acts of love anyone can give to another. His friend pointed out this killer's faults, and he did so very effectively. As the soldier rode proudly away from a successful church-destroying venture and on toward Damascus for another, his loving friend directed a bolt of lightning that knocked him to the ground, leaving him blind and speechless for three days.

As the story continues, we see that this great Roman begins to realize that the Christians are right and he and his Romans are very wrong. He also learns that beauty and joy exist in the love of God.

In his letter to us today, this great saint says, "Christ will be exalted through me whether I live or die, dying is so much gain. If, on the other hand, I am to go on living in the flesh, that means productive toil for me—and I do not know which I prefer. I long to be freed of this life to be with Christ, yet it is more urgent that I remain alive for his sake." (*Philippians 1:20*)

God continues to call to us as we build greater machines and energies powerful enough to destroy the world. He watches us as we fail to eliminate crime because man cannot change man. He bleeds as doctors kill babies and He stands aside as lawmakers forbid His name to be said in our public schools. Yet this peaceful message keeps working slowly and methodically until everyone will be of one flock. Even the greatest evils will give way to His tender will.

The Word lives in you. May you spread it by what you say and what you do!

GOD BLESS.

Love and charity bring peace through God…

Life flows smoothly and fills us with joy when we are enveloped in love and charity. Genuine love comes only with our association with God. Our feelings must exist for Him before they can be truly present for anyone or anything else.

In Matthew's Gospel today, Jesus says, "Whoever loves father or mother, son or daughter, more than me is not worthy of me." From these words we can imply that all existing matter belongs to the Father. It is on loan to us and we need to, with gratitude, treat it as such because some day we must return it. Our children and grandchildren are likewise His. They are gifts loaned to us for only a while, and we are obliged to lead them into life with this in mind.

God is love. He will not really exist for us unless we give Him freely, with no strings attached. This is what charity is. Love and charity are nearly the same and they make up the core of man.

Children born to parents of respect, who live in God, will in turn love themselves and be humble enough to become servants.

My friends, what else is life about? How else can man continue to exist? Today, with larger numbers of people wrapped up in the what's-in-it-for-me mindset, greater need exists for people like you with enough respect to use your talents for the good of God and his creation, and enough personal pride to forgive injustice and to see God even in those who bring pain. You know from your own lifestyle that more lasting satisfaction comes from giving.

The world belongs to those who let go and give it away. May you inherit it all.

GOD BLESS.

Face life head on for peace and joy…

Take care of things while they are small. Believe in God and have strong faith as He works through you. Know that anything worthwhile is difficult, sometimes extremely so, and takes your best effort to accomplish.

Today God tells us that the easiest and most fulfilling way through life is to face, head on, all the difficult factors. Many lives are failures because of life's challenges! Many die young because of physical or mental illnesses that our human knowledge and means cannot cure. Some die because of a destructive blow from nature, some through accidents, and many deaths take place because of the difficulties of everyday living.

We all need help. Usually a sympathetic friend is enough. Some require professional therapists, and some just can't make it. They must be taken out of society and placed in health institutions or in prisons.

How sad this is because we have the means and all the necessary strength inside ourselves. Many do not recognize this strength and their lives are filled with uncertainty, chaos, and tragedy.

In the first reading, Elijah tells us that he stole away to be alone and he looked for the Lord in the wilderness. (Here the Lord he seeks is a symbol.) He symbolizes the peace and tranquility Elijah needs in his hectic life as a prophet.

First he encounters a wind so strong it crushes rocks. He next encounters an earthquake, and then fire. The peace he sought was not in any of them. His story tells us that he did find a needed relief from anxiety—his Lord. It came to him through a "tiny whispering sound." When he heard it, he "hid his face in his cloak." His action here is also a symbol of what he really did. His

----

hiding symbolizes that he quietly abandoned all earthly thoughts and let God work inside. In that moment, he let go of all his troubling thoughts and let warm, peaceful feelings replace them. His former uneasiness became a quiet comfortable relief. This filled him with a new strength. Afterward he could go back out into the world and face the jeering, the mockery, and the threats from those who wanted him out of their lives because he pointed out their sinfulness and brought guilt to their consciences.

My friends, God's message here through Elijah's story brings to the surface a knowledge that we have, but that has become recessed in the back of our brain. Even though we need friendship, laughter, and parties, we will never find the necessary peace in drunkenness, revelry, drugs, or other sins. Neither will we find this peace if we put off or turn our backs on things we find difficult in our lives or jobs.

Think deeply about the message of peace Elijah found in the "little sounds." Our lives, we find, are steeped in massive constructions, deafening rock music, and rich exotic foods and beverages. Peace exists in the beauty of a flower, the smile and gentle touch of a loved one, the tenderness and innocence of a child, knowledge that we've done the best we can, and the list can go on and on.

God bless you. Hear the message of the great prophet. Enjoy the little things God has set around you. Take on your obligations. Solve problems while they are small. Then the world will be yours and everything that's in it. And you will be happy, pleased, and at peace. This is God's promise!

GOD BLESS.

Peace…All that is required is to slow down, look and listen for the spirit of God…

✝

Saint Peter, writing about Jesus, tells us this: "He was insulted and returned no insult. When he was made to suffer, he did not counter with threats. He gave his body to the cross so that all of us could live in accordance with God's will." (*1 Peter 2:23-24*)

Saint John writes these words: "I am the gate. Whoever enters through me will be safe. The thief comes to steal, slaughter, and destroy. I came that they may have life to the full." *(John 10:9)*

To enjoy life, we seek excitement, thrills, comfort, and luxury, along with peace, love, and harmony. These are opposing things, but because of our complex composition, we are capable of having them all. God put us together that way. Saint John tells us this in those words of Jesus above, that you may have life to the full.

The man, woman, or child who has learned his or her place in the world and wishes true beauty and worth has no trouble finding pleasure. Mostly we find it in elements that occupy space, can be seen, heard, and touched. God says, "Go ahead. Use them and enjoy life!" He created everything and he created nothing bad or evil. He gave them to us and the more one awakens to these unlimited elements, the happier and fuller life is.

Through living, however, we know that a life filled with nothing but thrills and luxury eventually brings boredom. Boredom causes people to become destructive when they seek more excitement, more thrills to replace those that are no longer fun. These people sometimes overdo and overuse, and there comes a point where use becomes abuse, and any degree of abuse is sinful and damaging.

People who slide into these habits have developed only their physical and social natures and are but two-thirds grown. Many of these eventually need therapists to help get their lives back in order. A few, unfortunately, rise to power. They over-demand, enslave, and sometimes cause others to turn to warfare. They create chaos and chaos brings only useless destruction. All this occurs because they never sought or developed the other one-third of their personalities.

They never learned that life requires a time to pray, to meditate upon where you are, where you are going, and whether you are in harmony with God and the rest of nature, or whether you've achieved your full beauty. They've never learned that to be whole and happy, one must use the world within its intended limits and only for the purpose for which it was created.

They have never developed their souls. They have never discovered peace though it exists right inside them.

It is never too late! We all have the means. All that is required to find it is to slow down, look, and listen for our inner beauty through the spirit of God. It only takes a little faith, hope, and genuine charity.

God bless you. May what you do be an example to young and to old of total humanity. The future of all we have depends upon you and upon me.

GOD BLESS.

With the feast of Pentecost the church rejoices
that Jesus Christ has not left us orphans…

☦

On this day our Holy Catholic Church celebrates, in memory, the climax of everything Jesus has given us and died for. This recollection is the Holy Spirit. It is the renewal of God in our lives. The presence of the Spirit is the promise that guarantees that Jesus, His works, and His words will never be forgotten. The Holy Spirit is the assurance that Jesus shall not have died in vain.

Two thousand years ago, there was much danger in the days following the death of Jesus. Today's gospel shows the apostles huddled behind locked doors, trying to make sense out of what happened on that terrible Friday. They wondered if perhaps they should just forget about him and go back to their old jobs.

This Jesus would never allow. He filled the room and their hearts with tongues of fire. They received the Holy Spirit—the Spirit that would never let them or anyone else called to the faith ever forget His words, His deeds, or the reason He died.

From that day on, every time we come together we renew the memory of Him. We pray together. We share the readings together. We break bread together, and from generation to generation, we pass on the stories of His teaching, healing, forgiving, loving, dying, and rising.

This day should remind us of why we celebrate Mass. It exists to renew our own enthusiasm about a flourishing, growing faith.

May the fire of the Holy Spirit make you glow with love. May your life spread the memory of all Jesus gave to us.

GOD BLESS.

CHAPTER 5

WISDOM

"Being wise calls for

common sense."

INTRODUCTION TO CHAPTER 5

WISDOM

God is love! Love is that quality that means all creation, including all people, are treated with fairness and respectful sensitivity.

God, we all know, created man and woman in His own image, and put into our hands the responsibility for the happiness and welfare of everything. As wise people, we learn and acquire knowledge. We become aware of how much and how rapidly all the elements in the world and we, ourselves, change. God made us His vessels. It is we who change with change, and it is we who enable everything else to move forward into harmony with the rest.

All of us who have lived some years have at times experienced stresses. We also know very well that over time we've also made good choices. We do, with God's help, work our way back up to peace and happiness. God, in His wisdom, has filled us with His holy spirit and stands beside us from where He will help us in the worst of times.

We, in our wisdom, have learned and know when we are helplessly in need. He will accept anything we ask Him to take. We need deep faith to do this. Do trust Him! Tell Him, "Lord, this is more than I can really take. Please, take this cross from me." I know this works. It happened to someone I love very much. God sent the help the person needed, this time immediately. He always sends His help. It comes in His way and in His time. God answers every prayer in His way, which may really not be the way we expect, but He does answer.

He is God of wisdom, who created and loves divinely every child, woman, man whom He has placed in His beautiful world, and He offers wisdom to us all. We have a need, though, to personally search to find it then to put it to use for the good of all.

---

1 John 3:2
"We are God's now,
What we shall later be has not yet come to light.
We know that, when it comes to light we shall be like him,
for we shall see him as he is."

☩

Here is a mystery. It is confusing, but filled with beauty. It is a promise, but not a challenge.

The promise is a guarantee, but not necessarily to happen as we expect. It seems to contradict itself, yet, like all knowledge about God and his covenant, it is a mystery too beautiful to not be believed.

To understand, one needs to develop as complete a picture of God as possible.

Think back about everything Jesus said and did while He was here. In John's Gospel, 10: 11–18, Jesus refers to Himself as a "shepherd" who is willing to die defending His flock from the wolf. He is known by His flock. The same way, the Father knows me, one who is willing to die for those "outside the flock," who will hear His voice and come to Him.

The pages of your Bible are filled with many such stories about what He did and said that give meaning to His seemingly contradictory words from today's gospel. A blind man came to Him with the request, "Lord, help me that I may see." In his desperate need he turned to Jesus, and because of his faith, his "eyes became opened."

At the pending death of Jesus' dear friend Lazarus, Mary and Martha called for Him. He didn't come right away. He came after the body had festered in the tomb. When He did come, Mary, with deep trust, said, "Lord, if you had been here, our brother would not have died, but now his body is decayed." *(John 11:21)*

He assured her and Martha that their brother would rise from death. At this point, He reunited Lazarus with his soul and brought him back to life.

Aren't these stories living examples to help us understand everything Jesus wants us to know? Sunday after Sunday He sends this same message, retold in different forms, because each hears it differently and in differing degrees of understanding.

Try as we may, we will not totally know Him in our lifetime, but try we must, and never stop. By doing so, in His chosen time, He will open our eyes and we will see. This is our challenge—yours and mine: His promise, His covenant, we have before us.

In order to grow in His wisdom and peace, we see here we have absolute need to turn to Him with our crosses and ask to "receive sight." It comes about slowly. By nourishing ourselves we move toward it, and we gain new understandings and new questions. This is the path of wisdom. Wisdom fills us with the light of "who He really is." We have His promise that someday we will really see who He is, and then we will be like Him.

GOD BLESS.

The Lord heals the brokenhearted
and lifts up the oppressed…Psalm 147:3

As I read Saint Mark's Gospel today, I got the feeling that during his life as a man, Jesus only wanted two things: first, to touch us with God's love, and second, to enjoy the total peace of uniting Himself completely with the Father through meditation and prayer.

By His teaching and works of mercy, He made God grow in our hearts and made His own human nature diminish.

People, however, would not, in that day, or today, allow this to happen. What we do is keep calling to Him to give us the things of this world we crave and reach for, and we accept, on only a very small scale, the message of His promise for peace and harmony that come only in the degrees that we open ourselves to them.

We get a picture of how it is between God and people. Jesus was on His way to Simon's house to relax with His friends and to make the love of God become alive in their hearts—like it was in His— and burn there in their hearts.

What He found was a very sick woman, Simon's mother, lying in bed with a terrible fever, dying. Knowing the desire people have to hang on to the world, He restored her health. The result of His act of love was that His message was overpowered by the act.

His importance as a giver and healer completely overshadowed His wish, which was to diminish Himself and to make God and all His beauty grow inside human hearts.

By sunset, all the people from town were at Simon's door; not to listen, but to bring their sick and possessed.

Jesus gave them what they wanted, and put His own wishes on the back burner. The consequence: His words about the most important thing in our lives were heard by only a few and on a very shallow level. From there it would grow, but would exist beneath the shadow of people's desire for worldliness.

The next morning, before anyone else woke up, Jesus silently walked far out into the desert, alone. He knelt in prayer, letting His spirit completely depart from the world and unite itself with the Father and all the hosts of heaven. He remained in this communion until His friends found Him. Even here, His closest friends failed to understand what they saw. They were the very few who were chosen to witness true and perfect prayer.

These men who loved Him saw only what the shallow eye can see. They interrupted His peace, telling Him that everyone was looking for Him. The public wanted Him to go back so they could honor Him and make Him the worldly hero He had become.

His answer was, "Let us move on to the neighboring village so that I may proclaim the good news there also. That is what I came to do." *(Mark 1:38)*

May the humility and wisdom of Jesus open the door to your heart so He may accomplish more deeply what He has come to do!

GOD BLESS.

John 20: 19–23
On the first day of the week, Mary Magdalene came
to the tomb early, while it was still dark,
and saw the stone removed from the tomb.
✝

The opening line of John's Gospel presents a picture of twelve holy hand-picked men locked in a room in Jerusalem. They were scared. They had witnessed a terrifying death and knew if they went out into the streets and did their job, they too would be crucified. Their fear existed because, like the rest of us, they craved the things of the world and were afraid of pain and death.

Look closely now to what happened when they turned to God. Suddenly, in the presence of the Holy Spirit, through His light, they understood themselves and were filled with faith about the unknown. Jesus' teachings finally became clear and they understood. They also knew they were to continue the work begun by Him and to carry it to the ends of the Earth. What He came to do was now finished and the rest fell upon them.

Look also at what happened to them when knowledge became clear. Their understanding of life and love and death completely changed. Their worldly life and personal security were no longer important. Instead, life in heaven and the presence of God, the spreading of knowledge, and having love replaced fear. There now existed great peace, which was the promise of their teacher.

On this holy day they began to boldly speak out against the injustices, wrongdoings, and the sins of their society against the working people by their rulers, who constantly taxed them to build up their own wealth and the wealth of their institutions. They condemned the sins of gluttony and impurity, and they came on strong.

As their minds began to comprehend more and more about themselves, others, and the world (the driving spirit of everyone), it began to come together for them. They saw, more and more, the entire picture. Their expanding knowledge made them aware what little they really knew about total knowledge. This realization also made it clearer what great beauty, peace, and love exists for those who open themselves to it.

Finally, material matter, including their own bodies, became less important. Fears about death, along with their other anxieties, disappeared.

God gives us all we need. His words point out the way. His son's life proved that peace and love can be ours even under the most painful situations. We need not fear the world or the unknown. We only need to turn to Him and answer in the words of a little Jewish girl, thirty-three years earlier, "Be it done unto me according to thy word." *(Luke 1;38)* Hers was perfect wisdom.

GOD BLESS.

Jesus, in His wisdom sees inside all hearts.

✟

Maryknoll Father, Jim Travis, shared a personal cross of early years in his priesthood. I recalled his story as I read today about Jesus' visit with the Samaritan woman at Jacob's well.

Father's story recalled working through the questions he raised concerning who he was: "Why am I here? Why was I born white?" He questioned that, perhaps, was meant to teach God's love in places other than his home. God had called him to Africa.

His words, along with Jesus', regarding the woman living in sin brought me to a shocking realization: God has a reason for everything we do and everywhere we go, and I must accept and love others as they are even though they may be offensive to me.

It occurs to me that God had arranged that situation specifically so Jesus would be there alone and the adulteress would be approaching it at the same time. God chose her to be His hands, His feet, and His lips to bring his Word to a multitude of extremely anti-Christian people. It was her story about her encounter with Jesus that caused them to listen and to believe.

From these two experiences we get wisdom, which leads to growth. No matter how badly I blacken my soul with sin, God's love for me does not dwindle. He still makes use of my hands, my feet, and my lips to cause others to find Him, to understand the beauty of Him, and to open their hearts to Him.

As new stories come to life for you and me, may we discover new powers in ourselves, and the powerful effect our words and actions have upon those whose lives we touch. And may we become aware that—even without trying—we are a vessel bringing awareness of God to vast numbers of nonbelievers.

GOD BLESS.

Wisdom 6:12
Resplendent and unfading is wisdom,
and she is readily perceived by those who love her
and found by those who seek her.
✝

Matthew's Gospel today calls one to look at the wisdom of the ways of God and man. Like last week's gospel, it has a surface story in which half of the ten maidens appear selfish for not sharing their oil with the five who didn't prepare for the long wait.

Also like last week's, He has a deeper message: He is asking us to open ourselves to wisdom, an ingredient for a successful and joyful life and the successful path to a joyful eternity. Those who earn space among the saints, by their wisdom, also fulfill their space here in this world.

Our first reading (Wisdom 6: 1–12) calls wisdom resplendent and unfading (unmatched in her entirety and never diminishing). She exists wherever we turn. She moves us to perfection, and she leads us to correct decisions. Obtaining her relieves all stress and she reaches out for everyone to grasp her.

So what is she and how do we obtain her?

First, whenever we become uneasy or react with anger or fall into serious sin, we have given up control over our feelings and our peace. The wise keep a hold on these. By knowing they are OK, they accept their experiences, pick them over, use what is beneficial to self and society, and discard the useless.

Second, wisdom forces one to examine desires and thoughts. The wise do not dwell on things from the past. Doing so causes anger, shame, or hurt. Instead, they use their experiences to solve problems of the present, creating the strength to move peacefully to the future with its new exciting challenges.

The minds of the wise are constantly looking ahead, anticipating each new challenge. They accept challenges for their value and enjoy the world and all it offers. For them, there is no boredom. Their minds continue to expand and they enjoy an ongoing flow of new exciting changes.

This is the message God gives today from the book of Wisdom and Saint Matthew's Gospel. Those wise virgins used past knowledge, applied it to the problem at hand, and their lives moved smoothly and successfully into an exciting new reward.

Those unwise five met failure because they didn't anticipate or analyze what they would need to make it through the period of waiting. They spent too much of their preparation time fantasizing about the joy of the upcoming events and didn't get themselves ready.

No one can prepare happiness and salvation for another. You alone must do it for yourself. You can find great joy and excitement in life's challenges if you move through each one wisely and look forward with excitement to new ones. It is also wise to meet and handle the most difficult first, then as time passes, you will be left with the easy ones. That is how each day should end.

GOD BLESS.

The wise men followed the star
and discovered Jesus!
✝

On Christmas morning, the baby and his parents were visited by the most humble, coarse, and unlikely men. As the story unfolded, these shepherds, became wise. This changed them so much they couldn't wait to tell the world what wonderful things had happened to them when they saw the Son of God—really saw Him in reality!

Later we celebrate the anniversary of the visit of three astrologers (learned men of science) who studied the stars' movement. They too came to see, knowing the holy baby king would be under the strange new star that hung above the holy cave where he lay.

Balthasar, Melchior, and Gaspar (the 3 wise men), found him, honored him, presented him with kingly gifts, and then went back to their homes. Like the shepherds, they were filled with peace and joy, and their lives became filled with wisdom.

As I read those stories and meditated on them, I found in our Catholic community many whose hearts are filled with the promised peace, love, wisdom, and joy that comes from knowing this baby and having encountered His presence within our hearts.

We are fortunate to have many members of our church community serve in ministries too numerous to mention. Your presence is felt. Some are seen. Many are unnoticed and un-thanked. You all come to the call of God to participate in the sacrifices and to refresh your hearts, souls, and your minds. Each time you serve, you plant another seed. The growth of your seed lies in the hands of God. You may never see its results, but you it's there and God nurtures it. You are building peace and harmony in the world.

GOD BLESS.

WISDOM

We must learn to be our own best friend because we fall too easily into the trap of being our worst enemy.

✝

The Sadducees attempted to make Jesus look foolish, like He was lacking wisdom. They asked whether or not He felt the people should continue to honor their king as they had always done. (The kings held a social position comparable to a god.)

He did not camouflage His words to spare their feelings. Straightforwardly He accused them of being hypocrites because they approached Him with compliments and praise then presented a question to which any answer would contradict His teachings about love and peace. He told them to give the king the honor due a king, but to give to God what He created man to give.

In today's gospel, the Pharisees approach Him. They come in a large group made up of the greatest debaters in town. They, too, feel that they can debate Jesus into a corner and make Him appear ridiculous. (Their society, like our own, had many laws and degrees of punishment to attempt to force the lowly people to live in harmony with the higher ups.)

They asked Jesus which commandment in that group of ten was the most effective by which man could be made to fall in line and stop their antisocial behavior?"

This, we see, is also their last question. His answer left no room for debate, and likewise no loophole for further questions. It was, and still is, the answer that cures all personal and social ills: LOVE! First of all, love your God, then, love your neighbor as yourself.

Before you ever say or do anything, give a thought to whether or not your response is pleasing to God.

Before you ever say or do anything with, for, or to your fellow man, ask yourself, "If he/she said or did this to me, how would it make me feel?"

When you forgive, you have love. When you love, you do not nurse anger or hatred. When your soul is freed from anger and hatred you bring peace upon earth and many with you to heaven.

This all takes *wisdom* from above.

GOD BLESS.

CHAPTER 6

FAITH AND HOPE

"Through faith and hope we see God's beauty…"

INTRODUCTION TO CHAPTER 6

FAITH and HOPE

A rainbow in the sky is God's promise He will never again destroy the world with water.

Being made in God's image means it behooves us to love life and accept His graces. He provides everything except determination. This is ours to provide, and it becomes easier as we continue to seek it. It increases more in His special creation, when we dispose ourselves to prayers and sacraments, which are all visible signs that give us the graces we need to face the day.

Treating people justly begins by forming the intention to do so each morning, then recalling and renewing that intention during the day. Examine how faithfully we are following this intention then seek to improve our efforts. When it breaks down, begin again. Do not abandon it. Making the intention is easy, but keeping and renewing them takes bigness.

Becoming discouraged by our failures happens when we do not understand the things that go on in our lives. We can do nothing without God. Turn to Him with our weaknesses. Then begin again. God promises to judge us more on our efforts than our failures. Our pride calls for success. This is why discouragement happens when we fail.

Being honest is being humble. When failures happen, beg God for graces, and then leave all else to Him. He will never abandon us if we keep trying. Our faults will slowly disappear as we practice virtue. We can best conquer insecurities by seeking opportunities to perform good deeds.

Joy and justice become habits of virtue when we do our part to live up to the messages He sends.

After many stormy days, snows of winter soften and are gone. Our gifts are warming sun, gentle breezes, and melting snow saturating the soil around us as the excesses quietly run into our lakes and rivers, and then empty into the seas.

We inherit gentle days. Lawns turn green. Sleeping trees fill with rising liquid food, and then tiny buds grow until leaves flutter in breezes. Birds fill the air with song as they mate, nest, and raise their babies.

God's beauty fills up the world! Man senses God and His work. Most of us lived in faith through the hard times and are now filled with hope. All is well! The unfortunate do not dwell upon God in harsh times.

GOD BLESS.

*Saint Paul states, "Present your needs to God
in every form of prayer and petitions…"*
✠

We have been blessed with priests who really love their priesthood. For me, they awaken awareness to truths about faith that have laid dormant in my life. I do feel a special gratification whenever I hear a homilist whose background and work is in history and philosophy. This always fills my life with hope.

On Saturday, I heard Fr. Whitney Evans, who teaches history and geology at Saint Scholastica. He showed effectively that it is not I who controls my life, but rather it is God. He also reinforced that letting go and allowing Him to work, opens me to His peace.

As all this passed through my mind, I recalled the words of another great man of God who had some solid advice for our world leaders. During those happy days when we saw communism crumble and the Berlin Wall fall, our Holy Father, Pope John Paul warned that planning to only replace one economic system with another it won't work. He advised that you need to give your country a soul."

All around us we see an ever-growing lust for power, riches, immediate pleasure, and a growing disrespect for human life. But men of God, like the prophets and apostles of the past, keep calling to us to let go of the worldly, turn to God with our pains, and know that in His time they will be made channels of peace for the world.

Today, the prophet Isaiah tells the story of an ancient grape farmer. He created a perfect environment for his vines, planted them, and then gave them the freedom to produce. They produced the wrong fruit so he let them go their own way. Weeds choked out the vines, the protective walls tumbled, and it became only a waste area waiting for someone to come along and restore it to productivity again.

Saint Paul is more direct in his letter: "Dismiss all anxiety from your minds. Present your needs to God in every form of prayer and in petitions filled with gratitude. Direct your thoughts to all that is true, all that deserves respect, all that is honest, pure, admirable, decent, and virtuous." *(Philippians 4:6)*

Matthew's Gospel uses Jesus' parable about the vineyard owner who leased out his vineyards and was to receive a share of the grapes at harvest time. However, those he sent to collect his share were ignored and shamed by the tenants.

The consequences for failing to respond correctly to their agreement with the master was, in the words of the priests and elders to whom Jesus was talking, "That wicked crowd will be brought to a bad end and his vineyard will be given to others who will see to it that he will receive his grapes at vintage time."

Except for the extinction of certain plants and animals and the onset of new varieties, the world has never changed. From the beginning of humankind, life has been a succession of the humble and meek producing leaders who get everyone working in harmony under God. New nations grow. After people become used to new wealth and comfort, they begin turning to worldly possessions and upon one another to gain more comfort and wealth. They turn away from family life, forget they are servants, become selfish, lose morality, and then decay as a society until the humble and meek again inherit the world.

I feel it is very safe to assume that the troubles between nations will continue until, like the forefathers of our early American nation, someone convinces the great leaders and their followers that peace will only come when everyone turns from hatred and killing and just trust in the hands of God. He is the one who will bring about the solutions in His way, in His own time.

Meanwhile, what do you and I do? We cannot, under our own human power, force peace, and neither can nor will anyone else.

We can, however, help bring it about. Remember the promise of our blessed mother at Fatima: "Say my rosary often. Offer it for the conversion of the world."

My friends, we have seen communism fall in Russia. You have been part of that. It will happen over and over. It has throughout history, and like all times, the meek and humble will inherit it all until all is accomplished.

God bless you. In humility, pray. Mention your needs. Mention all your friends and loved ones who have forgotten humility. They need you. Most of all, pray for the humility to give up earthly pleasures, especially those that may lead you to sin. The world needs you and all your humble ways.

GOD BLESS.

2 Kings 4:
"Thus says the Lord, 'they shall eat
And there shall be some left over.'"
✛

Hungry men and women are fed and filled by a miracle God worked through Elisha. A man from the community of believers came to the prophet with twenty loaves of bread made from his choice grain. To his surprise and disbelief, Alisha told him to feed the bread to the hundred-plus hungry people. He is surprised further when this small quantity fed the gathering and some was left.

In the book of John, this miracle is repeated. This time it is Jesus telling his disciples to feed more than five thousand people with five loaves and two dried fish. As before, after the crowd ate their fill, twelve baskets of the uneaten food were collected. John's story ends with Jesus fleeing to the mountains to avoid being forced by exuberant people to become their king. These types of successes are retold throughout the Bible. They have two messages for us.

First of all, they tell us that even the smallest amount of spiritual example we pass on to the spiritually starving satisfies their need and even provides some excess that passes on to countless many. Because so little goes so far, we are asked to share what we have. Even in our small ways, we count. We are extremely important. Whatever we give continues to nourish in unbelievably large amounts.

Secondly, it shows we want and need someone to lead us through life and in holiness. Every institution, every community, must have one person of good sense, fairness, and courage enough to listen to their people's wishes then give advice or even orders to act in ways that will stimulate growth.

We know from experience that if a leader is weak and changes his or her mind often, everyone in the community will act the way their leader does, and chaos will result. Because there is no unity or direction, the group falls apart.

The working poor of Jesus' were at the mercy of the barons, the revenue collectors, and all the powerful who forced demands upon them. Standing singly at the mercy of the rich, they needed and begged for a ruler.

They wanted a king who with love and fairness could organize them into a community with a common purpose and who was powerful enough to stand up to these domineering overlords.

With this picture, we can all see more clearly what is necessary for our own community. We need men and women who are big enough to stand strong against powerful demands. Groups clamor today for freedom to use contraception and abortion and freedom to go directly to God for reconciliation, avoiding the direct rule of the church to be reconciled. Use the confessional! Relax to the blessings of your confessor.

Some in our society are led to wishy-washy leaders who are more concerned with being popular and comfortable and not with justice. They live in great fear for their property, health and lives. Many form their own "watch dog" groups. Our media continually calls for more weapon bans, more police to cripple crime, and greater punishment for offenders who destroy the world.

Fortunately, God's voice is still heard and held to by strong people. These are the salvation of the society. They pass on the will of God. They win!

I pray that you—and I—will get on the winning team.

GOD BLESS.

Love and faith are giving and sharing the harvest…

----

*"Old age is the crowning point of earthly life,
a time to gather in the harvest you have sown.
It is a time to give of yourself to others as never before."*
                        ✞   *~ John Paul II*

Jesus chose His time to become man. It was a time known as the Pax Romana (one hundred years of peace in the Roman Empire). The Roman armies were not out conquering. All was conquered and under their control.

Since there were no new kingdoms to conquer, there were no sources of wealth by looting. The wealthy, however, maintained their high standards of living. This was achieved by making heavy demands upon their bonds people. These bonds people, the poor, scraped to live, and died in hardship and filthy conditions.

This was the time that the Son of God chose to come to Earth. His parents were poor, but his foster father supplied food and clean conditions by working long hard hours. These are the kind of conditions that cause men to die young.

At the age of thirty, Jesus began teaching. He spoke out gravely to the powerful about their abuses and assured the suffering that their rewards for tolerance and pure hearts were an eternity of peace and joy in His Father's house. Although life might bring want and pain, it need not bring sorrow. Learn to accept what exists. Give love and care to neighbors. He and His Father love all and will administer justice in time. The patient and the pure will enjoy eternal happiness.

Naturally, for this He knew He would be killed, but this beautiful news drew great numbers of people to Him. They pressed ever closer to hear His every word. He became, to them, a leader willing to die for their comfort and peace. He became their shepherd who led them to pastures of plenty and provided hope. He healed their bodies and raised their dead. They reached out to Him and believed His word. They became a nation who

---

abandoned the sin of idolatry. They were willing to give their own lives rather than offend their God of love.

The beauty of today's lesson is the knowledge that even though our loving Lord does not walk physically among us, He is always present, especially when we pray together, and personally in our hearts when we open up to love. He knocks on the door when our hearts go cold.

He assures us that justice will be done. There is a paradise for all who love and reach out to Him. We are also given to understand that all who see His son's presence will have peace on Earth and a place of never-ending joy in this paradise.

GOD BLESS.

"Goodness, like beauty, is in the eye of the beholder..."

✟

To understand the true beauty of today's stories, we need to look at a bit of Israel's history at this time. It was, we will see, very necessary for Jesus to appear upon the scene with His messages of peace and hope.

First of all, Israel was a nation sitting between the heathen powers of Egypt to the south, and Persia, Assyria, and Babylon to the north and east. And she was the battleground where most of the encounters took place. Also, since the time King Solomon ruled (960 BC), kings spent vast sums of money constructing elaborate temples and palaces.

Two classes of people existed: the very rich and the very poor. As has been the case throughout history, the rich basked in luxury. The poor paid extremely high taxes and worked as slaves in constructing these showplaces.

The poor existed for the luxury and comfort of the hierarchy. Their lives consisted of birth, slavery, and death. In our writer's words, "They lived in darkness."

My friends, imagine now, what happened in the hearts of these abused people when this man came among them with His beautiful stories of an eternity filled with love, comfort, joy, and peace after these few years they spent upon Earth.

They saw His miracles and heard His voice filled with tenderness as He told of a loving God whose greatest wish was to wipe their sweaty brow, lift the burdens from their backs, and let them recline in a cool place with peace. Imagine also their feelings when they heard Him denounce the powerful men as He stood face to face with them in the streets and avoided their traps through His cunning replies to their loaded questions.

Today's stories are of light coming into dark places. They portray the beauty of man's life when God touches it.

May God bless and touch you deeply. This week, when anger surfaces and tears at your heart, remain silent for ten seconds. The fingers of God will soothe the place where anger tore the fibers. Great peace will come. A beautiful light will brighten that moment.

GOD BLESS.

"If I just touch his clothing," she thought.
"I will be healed." Mark 5:28

✝

This poor woman lived with a steady issue of blood for twelve years. She spent all her money seeking medical help, and it only grew worse. The moment she touched Jesus' cloak, the bleeding stopped and she grew strong and healthy.

Jesus knew that His graces had gone out to someone. When He learned who received them and why, He uttered, "It is your faith that cured you." *(Matthew 9:22)* In His own words here, we have His unconditional promise. Why then can't you and I always get relief from our pains or find peace? This is also answered in these readings.

"God fashioned all things that they might have being, and the creatures of the world are wholesome; and there is not a destructive drug among them. For God formed man to be imperishable. But, through the envy of the devil, death entered the world." *(Wisdom 2, 24:14-15)*

If you and I could have total and unconditional faith, we would be in possession of peace, joy, and true love. As much as we try, however, we cringe and pull back when we encounter certain creatures and even certain people. Well-intended drugs become harmful when misused.

We are incapable of maintaining high degrees of faith in the knowledge that God provides everything we need for our well being. Biologically we know that when body cells die, our body rebuilds more to replace them; thus we should be built to live forever. But everything is worldly and everybody dies. Wisdom 2:99 explains why: "But by envy of the devil, death entered the world and they who are in his possession experience it."

As hard as we wish, as hard as we try to hold up our part of the covenant, the devil is there, and he does entice us to weakness. As long as we live he will exert some power, and our battle against his allurements will be constant. We will escape him, totally, only when we leave this Earth and enter heaven.

Life is filled with tough challenges. It stays beautiful, though, when we accept all that presents itself and when we avoid anger and self-pity. It remains beautiful for those with faith and for those who "know" that if they just touch His cloak they will be made well.

This is the power of faith. No one has it totally because Satan is around. Happiness and peace exist in abundance for us, though, when we listen to God's encouragements and when we help others to find faith.

GOD BLESS.

Because of faith, he could work miracles..."

Just what would it be like in our lives, if we chose to let go of all our worries about our security, give up our drive for luxury, and just live as Jesus did?

Jesus slept and ate whenever and wherever He was invited to. His greatest drive was to tell stories about heaven and about the love of His Father. His faith in God's love and in God's promises to provide life's necessities was total.

Because of this faith, He could work miracles. Greatest of all, He accepted all pain and even death. His purpose of being was to help us to learn to love and to enjoy holy peace. Might it be possible for me to follow a life such as this?

Saint Francis of Assisi was the son of a wealthy merchant. Finding tranquility in His love for God beyond that of the world, He gave all his inherited wealth to the poor and lived as a hermit and from day to day on what God promised.

The story of his life tells of a time when he couldn't get his mind off a worldly fantasy. He dashed out the door of his tent and ran into a large thorn bush, where he hung by his thorn-punctured skin, unconscious, until his friends pulled him off and nursed him back to health.

He founded the great order of Franciscan Fathers who devoted their lives to prayer and poverty.

Men and women today still make choices to live for God. They never want to go back into the world of luxuries and comforts. For them, there is peace like I can't even visualize. How hard we find it to let go, but great peace comes to those who do! We must, at least, put materialism in a proper place where it does not rule our lives.

Thinking back to my own boyhood on the farm in the 1930s, there were not many comforts. We spent our summer days working in the fields and with farm animals, tending their babies after the heat of a long day. We often sat outside in the coolness of the evening, just talking. We could look across the fields and enjoy the peacefully rolling fields of grain like slow giant waves on a lake. There wasn't much luxury, but we had true peace and true love was there. We were contented.

I wonder, sometimes, if heaven might be that way. It really isn't a whole lot, but it is enough. I understand, though, that heaven is all the beauty we've ever known, but multiplied hundreds of times. Samplings here do exist if we slow down enough to see them.

May God's Word trigger some special peace in you.

May you recognize the pieces of heaven that exist around you. That is why you were really created.

GOD BLESS.

"Come to me all you who are weary and
Find life burdensome…
…for my yoke is easy and my burden light."
~Saint Matthew (Matthew 1 1:28)
✟

Our world is sometimes gentle, but we know it is sometimes harsh and impersonal. We can lose our gentleness and fail to accept peace from the hand of God. Because worldly things surround us, we often turn to them for our gratification. As we reach out to them, however, we only find more calloused worldliness.

God works hard to touch us, but we often just don't recognize Him. His rewards are gentle, warm, and peaceful, but we sometimes miss it. In Matthew's Gospel, Jesus says, "Come to me all you who are weary and find life burdensome, and I will refresh you. Take my yoke upon your shoulders and learn from me, for I am gentle and humble of heart. Your soul will find rest, for my yoke is easy and my burden light." *(Matthew 1 1:28)*

Some writers inspire us to look into the hearts of people and into the heart of nature where beauty is present. They point out the beauty of the flowers and their perfumes, and the music of the birds, all for our inner pleasures. Becoming aware of these makes us a more "whole person." The more "whole" we become, the more fulfilled our lives grow, and herein lies our peace. The more aware we become, the more we find ourselves living within the guidelines of his "yoke."

His "yoke" is the beauty that surrounds us and the Ten Commandments that guide us. They are easy and light. They are refreshing and bring comfort as one's gaze turns from "self" to the burdens of others.

Looking deeper into God, we find greater joy in life and treasures for eternity. We also stop looking so hard at "my" fun, and work at helping others find theirs.

All these promises we find written in the pages of the Bible. All are attainable, and all we need to do is to listen as He knocks, and to open the door. The rewards are a refreshing lifetime and a joyful eternity from a very gentle and humble servant.

God bless you. Stop awhile each day to look, to listen, and to receive Him.

"THE OLDER I GROW, THE MORE I LISTEN TO PEOPLE WHO DON'T TALK MUCH."

~ Henry Ward Beecher

GOD BLESS.

CHAPTER 7

GROWTH

Through the Liturgical Seasons

Cathedral of
Notre Dame,
Paris
3rd Sunday of
Advent, 2013

INTRODUCTION TO CHAPTER 7

GROWTH

. . . Through the Liturgical Seasons of Advent, Lent, and Easter

God's gift of life means our time is filled with challenges. We must find ways to beat down whatever brings defeat. Happiness or gloom in our lives is a choice we ourselves make as we go through our journey to eternity. Challenges will bombard us, and for God's most loved creatures who choose to respond with gloom, life moves slowly from sorrow to more of the same, and life grows hectic. There is not much rejoicing and the question, "Why me?" gets asked over and over.

There are men, women, and children who laugh and celebrate what God has given them. The joyous meet their challenges and work solutions, knowing that God is there beside them. They know He offers all the strength and grace they need to overcome hardships. They remain happy because they trust God hears and answers their prayers. They have learned to sacrifice and reach out to others in need. They know whatever they have given and done to others goes out and then returns, many times greater. Thus, they make sure that the things they give are blessed and done in love and in joy.

Our happy friends know that God's blessings can only bring joy when they are shared. They also learn that by sacrificing little things, they can live without a lot and life is fuller and more content when they possess less.

God carefully chooses His church leaders, who go about leading, not telling, by their lives. They make not only the church, but also all of society grow and flourish.

As men and women do what they do, others see, and some will imitate their ways. Thus it is that great men and women of the church have decided that we all need special seasons of time to meditate more upon relationships and to sacrifice small pleasant things from our lives.

As we learn to let go and to discipline our desires, we gain moral strength and learn to see the incidents of life as occasions of excitement and challenge. We learn to be happy with trials. When the trial is the loss of a loved one, God sends many friends. All come forth with comforting words and gifts that replace our sorrows with joy if we open up to them.

Such times happen early each winter prior to the birthday and Epiphany of our savior. We call it Advent. Another time occurs just prior to the resurrection of our crucified Jesus. We call that Lent. If we can grow a little during each season, over time, many little bits of growth become big and we along with the world grow because we sacrifice.

Now, please hear my messages from our loving God during the blessed seasons of Advent, Lent, and the greatest, most joyful season, Easter.

GOD BLESS.

...Many people flocked to the desert to hear Him.
Because His message was of forgiveness and hope...

✞

For thirty-eight years I prepared for and worked in the field of education, with young people moving into their places in the world. School is only one small part of the complex web of influences that developing persons encounter.

As I think back, I realize that great amounts of time are spent preparing to do the things of the world, and much less time is spent working for eternity. One's life work also is part of eternity when it is done for the good of God and people. It becomes one more occasion of sin, however, when wealth and popularity become the major goals.

Our human weaknesses allow room for this to happen and sin slides in. Our human weaknesses also allow us to be drawn toward the spectacular and pleasurable. This is worldliness. It is very attractive and sometimes difficult to control. It is also the road to stress and anxiety. God wants us to enjoy His gifts, but we do need to know limits.

Just as there is a call from the world, there is a call from the Holy Spirit. It is persistent, and when one hears it, it keeps us from going too far.

Isaiah tells us that in his search for God and his peace, when his prophetic life became unbearable, he found peace in quiet gentleness. This is where everyone can find peace. This is where we need to go to attain it.

We never seem to completely accept God into our lives. It seems like each time we encounter Him, it is a new experience. We don't really make Him a large part of us like we do the world. We pray daily. Some gather at church during the week to share prayer. This is especially pleasing to God, and His presence grows in us.

Holy Mother Church gives us special times to concentrate upon our gifts of happiness and peace. If we use our advent to prepare for His birthday and more intensely for His second coming, we will find greater peace.

We devote a lot of time during this season in preparing for parties and shopping for gifts, which is good, because God wants us to enjoy His world. He also, however, wants us to spend time in quietness, sensing His love and passing it on, especially to His poor and suffering.

What a beautiful, clear Advent image of expectations Jesus gives us through His words in Mark's Gospel: "John was clothed in camel's hair. His food was grasshoppers and honey. The theme of his teaching was 'One more powerful than I is to come after me. I am not fit to stoop to untie his sandal strap.'" *(Mark 1:1)*

My friends, many people flocked to the desert to hear John, because his message was of forgiveness and hope. He promised them that a person was coming who would take away all burdens and pain and would fill their hearts with happiness. The man did come to those who sought Him. He relieves their deepest sorrows. He fills their hearts with peace. He prepares them for eternal hope with love. He calls everyone else to come.

We know He is here. We can feel His presence. Take time each day to relax and follow Him. Practice Advent.

GOD BLESS.

Be constantly on the watch!
Stay awake! You do not know when the appointed time will come.
✝

What I would like most from life is pretty well everything that it offers. This is the selfish drive of people, and before anyone can begin to understand himself or herself, he or she must realize this. This is a force as we begin growing, but grow and learn we do, to control this force. It is good for us, if we keep it in check.

The things of the world are physical, and so it is very easy to become worldly and materialistic. Early in our adult lives we tend to reach out for the physical, especially since we live in a world of many choices.

Through growth, however, the wise learn that even though we need some things from the world, everything it offers is only temporary, and the more we grasp, the more of things we need to satisfy our cravings. Sometimes these cravings lie in the form of attention. Sometimes it's power, status, and love. Again, the wise resist. They learn that true happiness only comes when we lighten up on status of self and use our talents and energies to promote health to our community.

Stable people grow away from the habit of trying to gain attention and admiration as they grow into their middle and older stages of life. They live more and more for their community and society; making society strong. They become pleasing in the eyes of God, who has to look upon so much self-centeredness and greed in His world.

In Saint Mark's Gospel, Jesus tells his disciples, "Be on guard constantly. It is like a master who travels abroad and leaves his servants in charge each to his own task. Do not let him return and find you asleep. Stay prepared for his day of return." *(Mark 13:34)*

Life is peace-filled for those who live for God and neighbor. They run into snags and snarls, yet through honesty and love, they find contentment.

The great men and women of history are not loved and remembered for the positions they held. Nor are they remembered for their claims of achievement. Their names are honored for what they did that survived time, and the things that survive through them. They made life and times easier for the people of their time, and for those who came after them.

As we go through these times of revolutionary changes that bring fear and stress, we search constantly for ways to comfort people. In evaluating our own growth, don't dwell upon the great things we have done. Keep looking ahead for ways to use your energies for the good of God's name and for your neighbor. You will become pleasing to everyone, gain self-respect, and the world will grow because you were here.

Advent is the time to evaluate you, seek humility, and radiate love.

GOD BLESS.

Be strong, fear not! Here is your God,
He comes with vindication. Isaiah 35:4

As I read the Advent stories, my mind drifts back to my childhood. When my mother expected company, especially relatives who were going to visit for a few days, the broom came out, along with the mop and dusting cloths, and the whole house became as spotless as she was capable of making it. Being one of the youngest, and there being only boys (five to be exact) at home, I was often asked (usually told) to help her. I was mostly her gopher (go-for-this, go-for that) and the air seemed filled with joy and happy expectations.

When the time for the visit came, everything was prepared to Mother's best ability. Everyone was ready. The guests always felt warmly welcomed and the days were joyful. Every waking moment was filled with doing things that were fun. Everyone shared what there was.

These early years present themselves because it is what Advent seems to be all about. Literature tells of the coming of a baby. The expected "guest" is to be the one who will bring love into hearts, peace to the anxious, and hope to the hurting. We celebrate by extensive house cleaning, decorating, baking, shopping and sending special notes of love to those too distant to visit.

Joy and tenderness fill most hearts. We also see different faces coming to church—those who come only at special times like these, because thoughts of Jesus warm hearts a bit higher and make us feel more humble and appreciative. Love is warmer to those who are givers. Christmas tends to take us a step closer to "pure" love.

For those who experience Advent with love and expectation, it will never be a time of the blues, because we find true joy through giving and God becomes the center of the celebration.

When we have this attitude, God too, receives the gifts He desires. The most gratifying gifts we can give Him are a soul washed white from sin and a heart burning with love and willing to give to others.

So, as we prepare for Christmas, let's make gift shopping a special joy, and wrapping along with giving a pleasure. And let's pray a little deeper, cleanse our souls, and give God a special, beautiful gift.

Enjoy this holy season! It is a blessed time of promises of love and new beginnings of lasting peace and joy upon Earth.

GOD BLESS

God gives us special times like Advent
to start anew our growth toward our Father…

Those days two thousand years ago in the holy lands were not a great deal different from our times today. We today have the same human drives as those people did. We all make staying alive and happy a first priority, and our lives grow out from there. With only a few precautions, staying alive is pretty well taken care of for us. Seeking happiness gets us into trouble. It was the same back then.

Then, as now, there were many constructive, positive people who labored and loved. There were also those who used the helping hands of the system and gave nothing back. There were the wealthy who made life comfortable for themselves and others. There were the poor from whom life has a hope. Many found peace in life by living it naturally. Many others sought happiness in constant celebrating, mind-altering substances, and sin.

Since the time of Abraham, God gave the world prophets, but He sent His son to help us find peace in life and a happy eternity. At the first post-Christmas, He sent Saint John the Baptist to prepare the way.

John was a striking person in his appearance and his eating habits. Many went out into the desert out of curiosity to see him. His looks brought them out, but his stories kept them coming back. He told about a certain man who would be coming among them. This man would touch each one in some way.

The suffering and those with heavy burdens He would lift from them and carry Himself. Those with guilt, He would forgive and take the uneasiness and also carry that Himself.

For the abusers who failed to repent, He would continue His call to repent and amend. To the poor and homeless, He would give thoughts of eternal joy in a home in heaven. For everyone He would die to open the pathway to that home. He will come back at the end of time to collect all the faithful to heaven and the sinners to eternal hell.

Then, as now, all heard, but turned to God in different degrees. Now, as then, He gives us such people as Saint John to make us aware of His presence among us and inside of us. He gives us special times like Advent to start anew our growth toward His father. He tells us to find joy in giving and receiving, and to radiate His love to the rest of His people.

As you prepare for Christmas, may you receive Christ's presence deeper and fuller in your heart.

Also, as you prepare for Christmas, take a minute each day to pray for those who have died from the hands of people filled with hate, for all who are angry, and for anyone who has died violently, especially by man's inventions. Also pray for those who suffer loss.

Give God a special thank you for those lives He spared and who have themselves, failed to see His loving hand protecting them. This is your charity.

Let's also pray daily for our media, who report violence and hatred daily, who encourage more laws and stronger penalties upon criminals and yet fail to tell the world about the messengers of love and peace and the large number of people who respond to this and whose hearts are filled with love.

GOD BLESS.

The Lord is with you. You are blessed. Luke 1:28
✝

Mary gave herself, bodily, soul, and mind to the will of God: "I am the maidservant of the Lord. Let it be dome as you say."

God returned her gift a hundredfold. He blessed her with the conception of a baby even as she kept her vow to resist forever the second most powerful drive given to people. That baby was God's own son, who is one and the same with Him in heaven.

We have learned throughout life, and especially as parents, that what we give is returned a hundredfold. It brings with it joy and peace, and a feeling of love that can never be equaled through earthly purchases. I find it impossible, however, to imagine what the feelings would be like if I were to totally divorce myself from the world and accept, without any resistance, what God asks of me.

How terribly painful and frightening were the times when Barb and I stood beside our son's hospital beds, praying, as they suffered on the brink of death. Mary watched her son being tortured. She saw His body continue to weaken until He was nailed to the cross, where He died. She totally committed herself to the will of God and not only received the graces to withstand this scene, but also the graces to forgive these heartless men. These graces allowed her heart to remain full of love for all of them.

God's commandments tell us that there is only one way to peace, happiness, and love throughout this life and into eternity. He sent and continues to send us those whose lives prove that this path is possible and even quite easy to follow. Its rewards bring all the happiness and excitement we want and need for a complete and full life.

Yes, we see things around us and we know better, but we are only humans and tempted at every corner to reach for the material

----

things others present to us for pleasure. We turn to these, and yes, it is OK. God provides everything. We must never forget, however, that it is our strong desires for worldly things and our uncontrolled drives to acquire them that bring stress and anxieties into our lives.

He continually sends women like Mary and men like Jesus to keep calling us back to our real purpose of using our talents to improve the world, sacrifice for the less fortunate, and relieve pains wherever possible. Only by walking this path do we find lasting happiness. This road alone relieves stresses and anxieties and feeds the heart with love.

His gift provides us with the opportunity to experience the pleasure of giving to others. His gifts are so many and so obvious. If, as we encounter them, we can see Him a little more clearly, and feel Him a little deeper, we continue to grow. This growth will only continue to multiply and we will not only experience a life filled with peace and love, we will someday enjoy it beyond our imagination, with all the angels and saints in heaven.

May Christ's birthday open your lives to continual growth in his promises.

GOD BLESS.

Feast of the Epiphany
Isaiah 60:1–6, Eph. 3:2–3, 5–6, Matt. 2:1–12
✝

I get fulfillment from learning the origin of practices and even how our words originated. Our Epiphany celebration originated in the Eastern church. The three star-studiers were from the east.

Epiphany is celebrated annually on January 6, twelve days after Christmas, and sometimes is called the twelfth night. These men were the first gentiles to experience Jesus in His glory as the Son of God. Knowledge of the glory of God's son began here and these three began to tell the story to the world. It precedes two other manifestations of His glory. It is followed by the events that happened at His baptism, then at thirty years of age, His first miracle at the wedding at Cana.

This epic story is summarized of course, shortened to keep the Bible down to size. We do not really learn who they were or where they specifically came from, but they raise meanings about the effects of Jesus upon the world.

First, these wise men found new light. They became intrigued and sought its meaning until its origin was found. The light symbolizes great and new understanding about God in us. New knowledge about Jesus, and all of heaven produced here a deeper, truer, and purer love for all that surrounds us. Here lies the real power of all God's gifts. It is here that peace and tranquility exist.

We see that trials exist on the path to the cradle of truth and love. The men encountered a jealous king who lied about wanting to also adore His replacement. After they found God's son, they learned the truth of Herod's intent. They did what they had come to do and then hurried away from that evil man who wished to kill that innocent baby, and likely his saintly father and mother, and them, too.

Thirdly, it is the story about human love. When these men finally found the object of their search, what did they do? They greeted Him with honor and joy, even prostrating upon the floor before Him. Today we show this same respect by shaking hands or even more deeply, with a hug or a kiss.

Their humble responses said to the baby, "I love you and here is how much." They gave Him valuable gifts from their possessions. And as I have asked myself many times why I give gifts, the answer is right here for us. Giving is really saying, "I love you!" This also says, "This is how much I love you."

God's love is portrayed in our giving. God's love goes so far as to say, "Whatever I have is yours. Please accept it!" And when your gift comes from your heart, you too are deeply rewarded. There is a happy glow in the ones you love and the whole world becomes brighter before you. Sometimes our gift is only a warm smile, but it does the same thing.

In this story we have heard God speak and the words are necessary. The world may hear it, but not all examine it. Such stories *must* be told over and over. We need to tell our young. They are taught, by the great institutions, to seek the facts that lead to wealth and power, but our church institution teaches that *real* happiness is quiet solitude and giving. This offsets the need for prestige. If we don't teach them these stories, these stories will die. Telling these stories will make the holy light of heaven shine forever.

GOD BLESS.

First Sunday of Lent

✝

Last week we were told how important we are to God and how deeply He feels about us. Saint Paul informed us that we are His temple, the vessel in which all that God does and is takes place.

Today we see how differently He made us from the rest of creation.

The world and everything on it occurred at his command. We were specially formed. In His hands he took the soil of His earth and carefully formed us then blew His breath into us. It is this breath that gives us life. How important, how beautiful we are to Him.

He put our first parents into a garden where He pampered them and provided everything, including eternal life. They were told to fill the world and to take command over everything it contained.

Adam and Eve failed, though. They misused the vessel of God and ate the forbidden fruit, despite having plenty of everything else.

This is how it is with us. We have all we need, and eternity is mostly what we are here for. However, like our first parents, we get intrigued with the attractions of the world and our own glory and then devote too much time to them.

God wants us to enjoy the world to the maximum. We should. We need to remember, though, the world is only a small part of what He gave us, and though eternity seems long into the future, we do need to grow constantly in peace and harmony with all creation.

Each year Lent causes us to recall the pain and suffering Jesus endured with love, for us. We are asked to follow our priest, bishop, and pope in sacrificing a small amount of the pleasures we enjoy. This will give us a little more control over our wills. This is how we can clean up His temple.

This Lenten season may you let go of some small pleasure and stay with this sacrifice for forty days. You will discover some very exciting facts about yourself and those who are close to you.

GOD BLESS.

LENT

It is very necessary to look back, not with a longing to return for that would only be fantasy. But to discover where we came from, who we are, and where we are going.

Since Lent began, the Old Testament takes us back into Genesis. It starts with Adam and Eve, Eden, and how God pampered them while they lived in total obedience and innocence. After they sinned, they became knowledgeable of good and evil. After choosing to allow evil into their lives, they had to endure the world, work for their food, and then die to complete the cycle back to eternal peace, beauty, and freedom from the devil and his evil promises.

Is this not also our story from birth to death? The rest of the Bible, the interpretations by our priests and other teachers, is about the fulfillment of this story. The messages are very subtle and demand undivided attention and deep concentration to really hear and understand them.

Good listeners hear the message that God is constantly asking us to act out of love and sacrifice. We also become aware that this is the only way to the deep peace that God provides.

This is the message today. At the age of seventy-five, Abraham, in obedience to God's command, left the land of his father and established his own place in a new land that God gave him.

This obedience resulted in his long life and uncountable descendants, including Jesus. He received all of this even though he and Sarah had just one child. This same message of love and obedience comes through Paul's letter to Timothy. He tells Timothy not to give in, but to stand up to all hardships because the Gospel promises that death will be overcome and we will be rewarded with immortality.

Saint Matthew describes these rewards through Peter, James, and John. These men, who gave so much, were permitted to see Jesus in full glory: "He became dazzling as light." *(Matthew 17:2)* Even though you and I still cannot fully visualize this, there is no doubt that this reward for a God-centered life reaches far beyond any beauty and joy that we can experience here. It is unimaginable. It is totally satisfying. It is without end. As you hear these stories about Him, may you grow a bit more determined to shun sin and reach for Him with the limited abilities He gave all of us.

GOD BLESS.

LIVE IN THE LIGHT OF HIS LOVE.

✞

Last week, Jesus said, "I am the light of the world. Whoever follows me will not walk in darkness, but will have the light of life." *(John 8:12)* Today, he implies, "I am love." He is depicted by our writers as having several human virtues.

In Saint John's Gospel, He cried at the tomb of Lazarus, tears of tenderness and sympathy for Martha, Mary, and their dead brother. Earlier, when He first heard of Lazarus's illness, He said, "This sickness is not to end in death rather it is for God's glory." *(John 11:4)* Words of hope as He is implying that we endure all for God that His name may grow!

He called Lazarus back to life. Here is His promise to those who hope. This is supported by Paul's words to the Romans, "If the spirit of him who raised Jesus from the dead dwells in you, then he who raised Christ will bring your mortal bodies to life also through this spirit." The resurrection of our bodies will occur. There is no reason to hang on to doubts.

The entire mood for these virtue allegories is created in the words of Ezekiel, "Thus says the Lord God: O my people, I will open your graves and have you rise from them. Then bring you back to the land of Israel." *(Ezekiel 37:12-13)*

When I read these words, I let go of all my tensions. I enjoy for a while that same wonderful feeling I used to have in my boyhood when with my good friends, that everything in the world is OK. No matter what one felt or said he or she is totally accepted and never prejudged. Those were peaceful times, and though only memories, they serve as reminders of how beautiful life can be when everyone gives the care and space to be free with God.

God, we are told here, loves us so much that He is actually going to open our grave, glorify our body, and take us forever into the city of Joy. He doesn't set any conditions here. He will go to each and every body to bring it home. The only cause that will keep us from entering will be if our soul is so blackened that when we see God in all His beauty and glory, we will not be able to accept His embrace.

Where will we ever find a better picture of love! No matter how much we have hurt Him, He will come to take us home. From this, we know that heaven is real and that we are dearly loved.

Let these pictures put your heart at ease. Let go of your earthly anxieties. Live in the light of His love.

GOD BLESS.

PASSION (PALM) SUNDAY

✠

"My heart is nearly broken with sorrow. Remain here and stay awake with me." *(Matthew 26:38)* As Jesus went to the garden to pray, He asked this of Peter and Zebedee's two sons.

If you have ever been blessed with a friend or loved one coming to you to unburden, you know the beautiful feeling of the—implied words. "I love you! I will bare my soul to you! You care and I trust you with my secrets!"

If you've never encountered this to any deep degree and wish to, there are two things you can do: Become warm to anyone who seems to be avoiding you, and when someone is speaking "to you," listen and listen intently.

When someone knows you really care, she or he will trust you and share his or her "soul" thoughts with you. The person will share, however, only to the degree that you listen and sympathize. When people let go of their sacred feelings, something wonderful happens: the two of you grow very close and you cleanse each other from pain.

Only a few are fortunate to have such a friend. Some are blessed in having that person in a son or daughter, or as their spouse. The people this close enjoy a deep trust in the sanctity of silence. What a beautiful level of achievement. You are walking within a degree of divine love and it is genuine.

We who were chosen to enter the Catholic faith are blessed with such a person. Our priest in the reconciliation room has been carefully hand-picked by God to be here for us. He has heard and will continue to hear the darkest sins and deepest pains. He maintains his oath of silence and loves deeply enough to never judge. What beautiful relief when he says, "By the power of God's grace, I absolve you from all your sins. Go and sin no more."

Beautiful feelings of relief come into your life when you unburden at this level.

Jesus, on that day, asked three friends he had such hope in to be with Him. How heartbroken and lonely he must have felt when he found them sleeping!

I ask myself sometimes, how often I have left people lonely and heartbroken when they wished that I would hear them?

When I fail in this, I, too, fall asleep when that person so desperately needs my comforting arms...for one hour. This is carrying Easter into everyday life. Listen closely. He usually calls through another human's voice.

GOD BLESS.

EASTER

When Christ our life appears,
then you shall appear with him in glory.

✝ Colossians 3:4

The passion and death of our Lord stands, for me, as a picture of a big man, a true leader, and one I can willingly follow. He is a person to be trusted because He is considerate of my fears and pains and helps me through the rough spots. He will risk His own welfare for us who follow Him.

A number of years ago, a president of a country gave an address to his people about the declining economic conditions. Prices had shot up and even the stock market failed to do good business for several days. Many people lost their jobs. In his polished, optimistic voice he said, "Everybody will need to tighten their belts for a while." Ten days later, the media informed the people that their president had flown, along with his advisors, to a Pacific island "for a conference." He also, the media said, used several planes to fly his bodyguards, and another to carry the two limousines they would need.

When Lent began that year a priest in a little country parish announced, in his homily, that the bishop would be doing a holy hour once a week during that season. This priest, too, said he would be doing this same extra service each Friday at noon. His words were, "Please join 'us' as we do this extra sacrifice to grow closer to our Lord."

Of these leaders, one leads for his own glory and comfort. His followers stand all alone with no one to guide them in their needs. The other puts himself into the shoes of the needy and walks with them. One makes the problems even worse. The other brings peace through his charity and love.

It is quite obvious that one of these institutions leads to failure. The difference between them lies in the fact that while the failing one is based upon worldliness and economics, the other is operating through his soul and he will continue to grow. The one with God at the center is followed by his people and his work will stand until the end of time.

Let us be thankful for being created into this institution of self-sacrifice and charity. Its final reward is eternal peace. When the worldly organization destroys itself, as we have seen in the case of the former Soviet Republic, the world with God at its center will find its way through the worst. There stands a promise: "The gates of hell shall not prevail against it." *(Matthew 16:18)*

My friends, God gave us guidelines, and in this story of Him during holy week, He shows us how it's done. And greater yet, He allows us to experience with Him the glory and joy that comes to one who silently sacrifices total self to the greatest pain that ever can be inflicted, and do so for the honor and glory of others and God.

May the growth you've made this Lenten season continue. May He bless you with understanding and help you grow in grace.

A while ago, television carried several stories about two modern-day disciples.

The first was a successful middle-aged business man from Kansas. He became so upset about the large number of men, women, and children who go hungry in our nation of overabundance and obesity, that he got on the phone, set up serving places, and got restaurants to pack their leftover food. Then he got delivery services to transport these parcels to where the poor could be served. The video went on to show how he expanded this service to other cities in the central United States. This formerly thrown away food now feeds hundreds.

The second was a young college graduate from New York who spent a year in a third-world country and now is working with and organizing others to work with people who have been involved in crimes in the inner cities.

One of our own, a doctor, took vacation time to do hospital work in one of the third-world countries.

These sacrifices of self give us hope. This is what keeps society going. These people "hear" the Easter message of God and live it out. His words warm their hearts like the two on the road to Emmaus, and like them, they recognize Him in the breaking and sharing of bread. For them, the promised peace exists.

Many of us are content to sit back and talk about what our government and social organizations need to do. It seems quite obvious to me that our governments are incapable of eliminating our social problems.

Our society will sustain itself only to the extent that individuals within follow the examples of the disciples. As more and more people stop extending hands that take, and put forward hands that give, we will remain healthy and flourish in peace and plenty.

The numbers of men and women who are called by God to become priests and nuns are diminishing alarmingly. The efforts of those who do answer will amount to very little if we fail to hear these calls, believe, and come forward. Our survival depends, not on the "other guy." It lies in the hands of myself and of you. America will continue to grow while we all extend them in service.

May "we" become more and more true disciples. May our hearts warm at His words, and may we break and share our bread. Because only then will we recognize Him.

GOD BLESS.

CONCLUSION – PART I

I hope and pray from deep within my heart that as I shared my feelings and thoughts with you, God found a peaceful place within your own hearts. May that grow slowly and warmly.

May the love within you swell and go forth into the hearts of all whom your life touches until it fills the world.

DEACON JIM

MESSAGES FROM THE HEART

PART II

THURSDAYS WITH THE DEACON

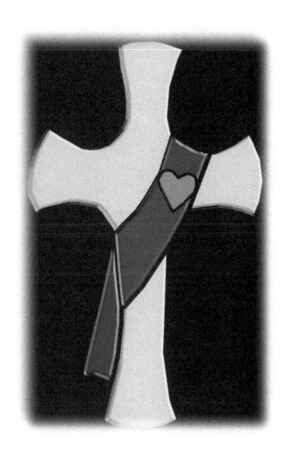

INTRODUCTION TO PART II

As I began my full time ministry at Saint Joseph's in Grand Rapids, I was given the privilege of delivering the homilies at the Tuesday morning liturgies (later moved to Thursdays). At that same time, the Way of the Heart group of women from the parish met immediately following mass and often times would "critique" many of these homilies. It is with their encouragement that I publish Part II of this book.

Each chapter is prefaced by a short "Message from the Deacon," accompanied by artwork done by my wife, Barb.

The Way of the Heart Women's Group

CHAPTER I

LOVE

Each day, may you find new love.

May your love produce more light.

May we all move toward your light.

And may all our lights illuminate the world.

A person who moves forward to what lies ahead…is a glorious light in a trying world.

Isaiah 49: 14–15, Matthew 6:24–34

✝

Today, Psalm 62 says, "Rest in God alone, my soul." Isaiah 49 shows us how it happens! "Can a Mother forget her child, be without tenderness for the child of her womb? Though she would, I will 'never' not love you with love divine!"

We, the fortunate, have lived in the arms of a mother's love. For eighty-two beautiful years I have seen, and love to witness children fondled by their parent. It touches my heart to see Mother or Dad lift up their child, giving them confidence to look upon the world and know it is OK. The child feels, "Because I am loved, I love it all too." How consoling to my soul when I see these children wrap their little arms tenderly around the neck of Mom or Dad, and let their little bodies rest entirely upon their parents.

This is human peace and love at its best and the little child bonds to that loving woman and that loving man. No matter what distractions may come from the outside, there will forever be a love between these parents and their son or daughter. As the children grow up and leave home, that love does not die. It only grows, and as they had been loved and treated, they too, will pass on love and this love reaches out to all the world.

In the Old Testament, Isaiah carries a mother's tender love forward to God's never-ending care for you and me today. Though no human love can come close to God's divine love, we do know and understand that God's tender love even exceeds a mother's. The beauty of our next life goes far deeper and richer than earthly love. Here is a calling from our loving God forcing me to walk around in His love letting it soak in and comfort me. The bond, the connection, the care, the tenderness of God for you and for me is far above any we have known. I only need to let myself feel it more deeply.

Changing to let God come into my soul is not complicated. It is simply trust; trust in Him at all times. Psalm 62 says, "Rest in God alone my soul. He alone is my rock and salvation." Oh! How I seek rest and comfort in so many earthly places and things. Yet, I only need to say in temptation situations, "Rest in God alone my soul." Just rest. Just let go and find comfort and care in God alone, instead of any other escapes.

He will take away my worry about all eternal things giving me freedom. He is telling me, "Don't be caught up in 'things.'" I will not be able to hear the cry of the poor and reach out to the needy and lonely if I am caught up in the things I want.

I should use those things that help me achieve the end I was created for and shun those things that get in the way of fulfilling my purpose. His wish is that I choose freedom and balance in my life with the things that achieve that purpose.

Jesus said it so wonderfully: "Seek first the kingdom of God and all these things will be given you besides." Chaos does not show its head in my world when I live simply.

GOD BLESS.

Hosea 11:1–4, Matthew 10:17–15
✝

Hosea creates a very beautiful and vivid image of God, one of a totally loving parent. This is the type of material I enjoy dwelling upon: God's great care for us, His "children," the picture of a totally loving parent. Hosea's letter is filled with faith and forgiveness through God acting as our parent; creating calm for his readers.

Matthew's Gospel, likewise, portrays vivid imagery showing Jesus sending out His apostles who have been endowed with great power to drive out unclean spirits and cure every disease, including cleansing lepers and raising the dead. They are to go out, though, with no money, no backpack, to walk those rocky roads of Palestine without sandals or a walking stick. They are to live entirely upon room and board from those who take them in. Their healing and delivering from evil spirits brings to light for us that this, now, is God's final reign over his people and his world. We have His holy word and His apostles to lead us on.

His apostles, including ourselves, are to do exactly what Jesus did, except we are to carry His message out to the entire world.

Just what are we to make out of God's planned efforts? He sent ill-prepared speakers out into the countryside doing what Jesus did. They were poorly equipped and dependent upon the hospitality of strangers. God is calling us to be missionaries or stay-at-home disciples. Following our risen Lord is a special, personal journey to us with our "ups and downs," our grace, and our sins. We do get changed by the encounters.

To encounter someone is a far deeper experience then just being physically next to him/her. My very deep life-changing encounter came many years ago. I've told about it before. It is still such a clear picture today and it changed my life a very great degree. As a young lad I stood by watching my mother give her tearful good-

---

byes to her sons who were leaving that day to go to the World War II war zone in Europe. She and all women were created uniquely by God to bear children and then to love their families far deeper than anyone else can. You women, made so by God, need to be loved, admired, and nearly adored for who you are. From among you came the Mother of God.

Our encounter with Jesus, just like with our mothers, can be filled with warm emotion and love given and received. It can be a love relationship mixing together care, concern, forgiveness, and love without limits.

We encounter Him in others—those who love us as we are and in those who try to change us. We encounter Him together in Eucharist.

Let us pray that we may continue to respond like all His disciples, sharing ourselves and Jesus, with all we encounter in our human family.

GOD BLESS YOU.

1Kings 18:41–46, Matthew 5:20–26
✝

Matthew's Gospel is about decaying elements in societies throughout the world and the sin of misdirected anger.

Never forget that properly channeled anger is of great benefit to creation, just like everything else God has given us. It *must* be nonviolent, though, like that of the world-changing people Martin Luther King Jr. and Mahatma Gandhi. But, there is no room anywhere for self-centered rage. We have all, at times, channeled anger to a productive and healing end.

Matthew recalls for us, today, the angers of our common present time. We have road rage, school shootings, Vladimir Putin, airport security, and, above all, stupid situations involving angry sport fans while enjoying their favorite athletic games.

Everyone knows that faith condemns murder. It also forbids all anger toward our neighbor. As our population grows larger, so do the numbers of people whose greed drives them to seek wealth and power and space.

So, what can *you* do to help clean anger out of our world? The same as I can! I can work hard at commandments one and two that lead me to open myself to God's love—which is not physically before me like my human friends and neighbors are.

It may seem like it would be easier to love my friends than God because I see them. However, they are also the people who are more likely to bring stress into my life. It is not God who tramples my flowers and who invades weaker countries.

It seems a lot simpler to approach His altar than it is to have a meal with those who have offended me, or whom I have offended, and to negotiate peace.

But God is adamant: I must settle with my opponents before I can go to God. The Gospel refers to the Scribes and Pharisees who were big on the "letter of the law" and "correct behavior." But Jesus pointed out that it is the *spirit* of love and reconciliation that stands at the top of all else.

The word reconcile comes from Latin and means to bring together again. As we go through this day, let's look for opportunities to manage anger, mend wounds, and get back together with those we are at odds with.

GOD BLESS YOU.

1 Corinthians 1:1–9, Matthew 24: 42–51
✝

The stories God comes with today plop our end of responsibility right onto our own laps where it belongs. We, again, are shown that God's hands never stop doling out graces into our very being, but often they fall worthless and unused. Matthew's Gospel gives us a command: "Stay awake because we don't know the moment of his call. No one knows!"

God gives us this scene: A householder wanting to catch a thief, but not knowing when he will attempt his trade, causes the making of some clever plans by each.

Next picture: The householder doles out responsibilities then leaves. The solution needs full attention. We must stop the enemy's attempt from damaging the owner's valuables and also be "awake" and waiting when he returns to again enjoy the belongings he possessed and entrusted to us. No one else can do this assignment except we to whom the responsibilities have been given!

Yes, God keeps his end of the covenant. Saint Paul explains in his letter to the Greek city of Corinth that although they accepted to live with the obligation of their conversion, they are now turning from their promise. In large numbers they are leaving their watches to take care of themselves abusing God's beloved creatures, and all he has created and left for us to keep healthy. They are misusing these things of the world for their own instant pleasures.

Paul reminds them that they have been given a world full of beautiful blessings. Paul sends his own blessings of God's graces and peace. He does not scold or condemn. He sends that which is best for them, God's love and peace, and sends this in sufficient amounts to heal many of their failures' sores.

For us to understand our own place in correcting people's shortcomings we see here the power of authority Saint Paul possesses with people. He uses only his holy capacity to demonstrate that he has "great" love for those who are challenging God and that he feels deeply disappointed in their poor choices.

Grace, peace, and other gifts given to us through Jesus are not simple presents that automatically become part of us. They are only resources that we ourselves have to use as we reach out to others. Love and warmth from us is just like from God; they open hearts and allow God to come in.

All people will know that God is love because of the love they see in us.

GOD BLESS YOU.

Acts 8:26–40; John 6:44–51
✝

As I searched through comments others have offered about these readings, I found this story that fits so well, concerning human feelings as the most sacred part of our personalities. It was touched upon in that small amount of time Philip spent with the God-seeking Ethiopian official.

In this story, a student hopes to stump his teacher by asking her, "What is the difference between teaching and educating?" He was struck by surprise at her response. She said, "A teacher passes on useful information for you to use to pass a test. The educator is one you meet years later at your class reunion and you say, 'I don't remember much of what you taught, but I'll never forget how you treated us and how you made me feel.'"

Today's gospel has a short phrase about living bread and how it leads us to a healthy feeling about faith and eternal life. It says, "They shall all be taught by God." Let us note that God teaches by doing. What He does, what He has done through His son, Jesus teaches us. Jesus leads us to our feelings.

Isaiah, in the Old Testament tells us that Zion will be restored by God and become again a place of peaceful gathering, worship, and blessing. Jeremiah speaks about God acting in love in the new covenant.

John's gospels speak of the Father teaching anew through Jesus. In them, manna from Exodus becomes newly alive, bringing fulfillment. Though he doesn't include the Last Supper story, he shows the unforgettable peace-giving acts of Jesus washing the feet of his disciples. This humble show of love then leads us to His ultimate loving act of dying on the cross and the cleansing that it brings. He teaches through doing and tells us, His followers, to do the same as we educate in His name.

The Ethiopian royal official is a good example of actions that bring joy and love. He, like all his people, is physically attractive because of his less dark skin and how he, and his people, cares and loves for everyone. He's deeply focused on carrying out God's example as he is trying to understand the passage from Isaiah. Then after Philip's words to him, he asks to be baptized.

As God's symbol he can say, later, of the caring disciple, Philip, "I'll never forget how he treated me and how I felt after he left me."

GOD BLESS YOU.

Jeremiah 1:4–5, 17–19; 1 Corinthians 12:31–13, 13; Luke 4:21–30

☩

In the past, some Native American people had a rite of passage. When a boy passed into manhood, on his thirteenth birthday, he was escorted miles out into the forest. As the sun was setting he was left alone to face the night. Darkness set in and he faced the unknown and the unseen with only himself to rely upon. Filled with noises and animals howling, the night seemed endless.

After enduring the night without sleep, dawn broke. Changing from a feeling of near panic, it became quite pleasant. Majestic trees swayed, colorful flowers bloomed on the floor, while wildlife searched for food. It was beautiful.

To his surprise, as the light grew brighter, he saw a male figure only a few yards away from him. It was his father. He had been standing there all night long, ready to protect him in an instant from the perils of the forest.

My friends, could this be your story? Crisis may sometimes drive us to the brink of panic, but when the crisis is past, the world becomes calm and filled with relief. It is beautiful beyond all the wonderful world we knew before. And standing nearby is the being who gave us the grace to hold out during all the fears and pain until we worked our way into the dawning of peace and comfort.

Today, we are in the dead of winter. The wind blows cold. You and I make a choice. We can choose to dwell, in mind, upon the clouds overhead and the sting of cold air, or we can use our time to say a prayer for our loved ones near or far, for our neighbors, or for a deceased loved one. We can use the time to invite your neighbor in for a visit at your table, have a cup of coffee or tea, perhaps something a little stronger.

Inside, we can be filled with peace, knowing that God will again soon send the warmth to melt the snow and awaken the resting

---

nature that surrounds us. The tender life of spring with its fragrant flowers will be returning, also birds, whose songs fill the air. This is really not far down the road, but we first have to find solace in the cold of the present.

We know that all things of life rest in his caring hands. Winter can be a fitting time to pray and to allow ourselves to become more deeply aware that the Holy Spirit is present to protect us from the blues. The Holy Spirit shows us that we are God's children and we have the power to be warm inside and filled with joy. Then when we meet others we will radiate this spirit of joy and love and this sends more peace back into our own hearts.

During these short, cold days and long evenings, the virtue of patience will become our mark of a healthy character. With this patience, we learn to accept others just as they are. This is love. God is love and we have it right inside ourselves.

Love does not sit still. It goes out to others and it forgives all and is merciful. Correctly handled, everything and everybody around us creates a more beautiful life.

GOD BLESS YOU.

Our readings today deal in deep metaphor and they show the apostles bewildered and confused. They have no idea what Jesus meant when he said, "A little while and you will not see me. In another little while you will see me," *(John 16-16)* . . . and he does not give them an explanation. This is typical of Jesus because to leave some questions causes people to think and reason and to talk about it. Then each interprets the information in his or her own unique way. This shows us that the speaker (and here it is Jesus) gives us the freedom to think uniquely.

Today, Jesus went up to his Father and again, His disciples are confused. They stood on the mountain staring into the sky until an angel told them to quit staring into the clouds and get to work. We have derived a saying from this: Get your head out of the clouds, your feet on the ground, and get real.

The mount of Ascension is like all the other mountains referred to in the Bible—the mountain of the Sermon on the Mount, the mountain of the transfiguration, and others. Their importance is that they are places where humans got to know God better. In the same way, what Jesus said is not as important as what He implied: "Get your head out of the clouds, your feet on the ground, and get to work at what you are commissioned to do." Like the apostles, we see that our missions are limited.

Here again, the mountain experiences show great power. It implies that the early church would not have survived, let alone flourished, had the disciples not "pulled their heads out of the clouds" and began, with great determination, the work to which Jesus had called them.

This also foreshadows that much work is still out there and has to be done. Where are our heads? Where are our feet? We all have a calling from God, and if we don't do it, knowledge of Him does not spread. It does not come so much from preaching as from the way we live our lives. Love and peace spread from our simple, everyday dialogue and from our everyday habits. Just take time to think about what you may have said or done. You affect the ways and the thinking of everyone who hears and sees you act. True feelings and body language pass your messages to everyone around you. You are God's vessel. Yours is God's wisdom to the world. Pass it on. Let it be peace, love, and happiness.

GOD BLESS YOU.

Acts 15:7–21, John 15:9–11

✝

We have all had sad experiences with saying final good-byes as we buried loved ones, whether it was a parent, perhaps a spouse, or a child. We know the pain of final good-byes to those we love. One day, we too will come to the end of our journey. What will those last moments be like? Will they be full of regrets? Fear? Hope? Joy?

Jesus' words to His disciples on the eve of His death are words of joy. He knows all the pain He will suffer, but His focus is not upon Himself, but upon those He loves.

Jesus spends these last days preparing his disciples for what is going to happen to Him before He returns to the Father. He tells them that one of them will betray Him to His tormentors. He tells them that they will all abandon Him. And he sums it up with the words, "I have told you this so that my joy may be complete." *(John 15:11)*

This picture should recall the sadness of our neighbors who have lost all they owned through storms and floods. Some even lost loved ones. It behooves us to reach out to them with charity and love. We will be contacted for charity and giving, which we all will do. We do, however, need to be sure that we donate to well-known charitable organizations.

We can be sure that there will be phone calls and letters to send money to a post office box. These are scams. Honest organizations we are familiar with will also contact us. Our loving care sustains lives and happiness, so we *must* give with joy, just as Jesus went with joy back to Bethlehem. He offered Himself to suffer and die and to rise so that we can have joy eternally and to be first to rise bodily and to ascend to our souls.

After His horrible grief and death, He rose, body and soul, and walked with His apostles for forty more days. Then He ascended to eternal joy. He wants for each one of us, and prepares us, to have the same eternal happiness.

His rough-natured fishermen apostles had learned to live lives of love, like Him. They also knew they were not going to have lives of pleasure and leisure in the world, but would have to say final good-byes, to struggle, to give even when it hurt, and to leave everything and everybody they knew and loved and to do so with love. He assures us, here, as He did them, that if we seek our happiness from things and people, we will not be fulfilled. Observing God's commands makes men and women complete, and through them true joy and total completeness happen.

GOD BLESS YOU.

Exodus 40:16–21, 34–38/ Matthew 13:47–53

✝

Need and change go hand in hand. Today our tabernacle contains the living body of Jesus. In our old church, the host was, and still is in many, placed before us in our sanctuary. We also remember that this sanctuary was just that: a sacred place where only the priest and specially trained male servants were allowed. The communion rail locked us away from it. Back then, communion was received only occasionally, because we needed to first confess our sins to be worthy to take Him into ourselves. This was the teaching of the church and we believed and we obeyed.

Today's letter from Exodus shows why this is the way. According to divine directions given to Moses, Moses built a tabernacle at the foot of Mount Sinai. Its purpose: to contain the presence of God. This sacred tabernacle, a tent, was enclosed by a cloud. God was present among them. As long as Moses lived, he alone was allowed to enter.

The holy writers must not be missed here. Moses received the Ten Commandments from God on this mountain. He placed them inside this tent, and God came down exactly as he does today through the hands of our priests. He dwelt in their sanctuary and in ours. He was carried by the Levites wherever they went, remaining among them.

The first half of their journey was very hard. It was filled with conflict and misunderstanding. The rest of the journey to Canaan began anew with the Lord leading the way as the Levites carried the Arc of the Covenant before them.

As conditions have changed, so have customs. People do not move en masse any longer. We build permanent gathering places and base our practices upon the knowledge we have.

Our hierarchy, our church teachers, have made changes through the second Vatican Council. After considering all men and all women are created in the image of God, the communion rail came down inviting us to participate within the sanctuary. We are invited to receive Jesus at all masses as long as we are free from mortal sin. The tabernacle containing Jesus may be placed in its own holy area apart from the Sanctuary. We are invited to visit with Him for an hour any time, when Mass is not taking place.

You and I are invited to solemnly take hosts from the tabernacle, place them in a special pix, and take them to shut-ins. We ourselves receive Him, newly consecrated, at Mass.

All Christian people are called to be instruments of God. We are His special image created to bring His love and kindness to the entire world. We are to bring them to everybody that He created. He has given us life on His Earth with only one command: to take His yoke upon our shoulders. It is light! It is sweet! It requires only that we give and bring joy to all the rest.

GOD BLESS YOU.

Jeremiah 18:1–6, Matthew 13: 47–53
✝

I think we all know that classical stories continue because they tell of the same conditions and occurrences that happen today.

It was 650 years before Jesus came to Earth that God sent Jeremiah to a small town near Jerusalem to that center of Judaism. He went before the Israelite leaders, their kings, to warn them of the power of God, which they had forgotten. This power was the very force that had willed and put into place everything that existed, including their very selves. He told a story of God's universal power, his law that governs the simplest forms of existence on up through every step in life, all the way to people. People were his most intelligent and complicated creations. He charged people to rule it all and make all things work for the well being of everything.

God knew that His super beings would need devoted men and women to bring them back into their natural order of peace. Some people would always have a drive for power and control over others. Sin befalls people when they begin to think of themselves as the power that will lead the world to its destiny.

Erring people from the beginning of humankind have made choices to worship their own hand-made items. Some chose the sun, the moon, or huge natural items to be their gods. Our holy creator, though, has never stopped sending specially chosen men and women to show them their folly in these practices. Especially distasteful were their practices of heinous and torturous sacrifices of innocent humans to appease their jealous, easily offended gods. Idolaters lived in constant fear of these false inventions of theirs.

Likewise, we today, invent gods and machines and then fear them. The sharpest minds among us do not know how to keep our discoveries under control. Because of this, we continue searching

----

for new, more destructive machines that will frighten others into obeying our wishes. Our leaders flaunt these machines to keep life safe for them and to make others weaker.

In the face of all of this, God has never stopped His quest or subtle ways of calling. Today we hear, "Like clay in the hands of the potter, so are you in my hands."
(Jeremiah 18:6)

There is a way to have peace, and it is extremely easy, just like our Jewish predecessors two thousand years ago. Devote one's self to that same silent and gentle voice that comes from your heart.

GOD BLESS YOU.

Isaiah 26:1–6, Matthew 7:21, 24–27

✠

The first reading uses gates to ancient cities to describe security for the people of those communities. The Gospel talks about a house with a firm foundation to depict a place where its occupants can have peace and safety.

That old saying, "Charity begins at home," wisely tells us that society is only as healthy and as good as the homes that make it up. These thoughts help me recall the words of Harvey Shew, my high school football coach, who long ago and often, told us that a football team is like a chain. It is only as strong as its weakest link and the boys who played for him played hard, but clean. Now, many years later, his wisdom is true for all of society.

This raises, for me, these questions:

- Am I becoming the best version of myself I can become?

- Do I delay my own gratification where necessary to gain control over myself?

Being simple and humble allows me to best serve more people! I must, daily, for the rest of my life, provide answers to these questions:

- How do I live?

- What is the best way for me to live?

- Do I believe Jesus gives me these ways? If not, who does?

- Do I help others find the best way for them to live?

I very greatly need faith, because heaven is real. Every good thing we have was given from heaven, and everything good leads to better—and then, a *best*—way.

Hell, likewise, is genuine. Many years ago, our Blessed Mother appeared to three children. Besides many happy things, she allowed them a short vision of the eternal fires burning in hell. They also saw some poor souls floating in the rolling eternal fires. This frightened them into a deep fear.

God created everything good, through love. He created us to live, forever, with Him in heaven full of wonderful surprises. Surprises like how much we are "really" loved, and how truly *loveable* we really are.

As you and I live, God wants an intimate friendship with us. It is absolutely necessary that we work to become the way God created us to be, 100 percent. This demands honest, daily examination and prayer.

GOD BLESS YOU.

CHAPTER 2

CHARITY

With each home we have lived in
we have left a garden!
A garden that grew nourishment for family
and friends, and a garden that filled the
landscape with beautiful flowers.
A place visited by butterflies and birds, and
gave happiness to so many.
A charitable gift to God's creation.

2Samuel 7:4–5,12–14,16; Matthew 1:16,18–21,24

✝

Joseph is a special person to me. When I was a toddler, my brother, in his early manhood then, had been named after the foster father of Jesus. He treated us, his younger brothers, very kindly. I always admired him and even imitated his mannerisms. I added his name to mine at confirmation.

Saint Joseph, I learned early in my life, is the patron saint of purity for men. All single men, husbands, and fathers can look to him when faced with temptations.

Married men who follow Joseph as a symbol of their respect for their wives and children will find as their married love matures, they grow to understand that God actually created us for one another.

The complete health of all children depends upon the true and gentle love of their parents. Also, true Christian parents lead their children into their virtues. Children are very fortunate if their parents set policies for them to live by.

As mothers and fathers, let us never forget that no matter how wealthy we've become, how successful, how much power we may wield over others, no matter how "smart" we feel we are, we must never try to replace God in controlling the world.

God is in charge. Hell will never conquer His will or His church.

And…when He needs human help, He chooses the humble. Their hands are ready to feed the hungry, clothe the naked, and shelter the homeless.

Jesus promised to return a hundredfold what you have given or shared with His less fortunate. The return is not always immediate, but it never fails if we have faith and "know" that it will.

When you visit with someone you don't enjoy being with, or listen with sympathy to someone's complaining, have faith. In time your charitable act will return a hundredfold. What a wonderful example for your children.

GOD BLESS YOU.

Acts 22: 30, 23: 6–11, John 17: 20–26
✛

In the early days of country music there was a song with these words: "You have to stand for something or you'll fall for anything!" *(You've Got to Stand for Something, Aaron Tippin, RCA Nashville, 1990)*

This crossed my mind when I read today's Epistle and Gospel.

First, Saint Paul brought chaos and dysfunction to the Sanhedrin. He stirred up a dismantling argument between the Pharisees and Sadducees that made them unable to decide what to do to him for preaching Jesus' words. He said, "I am a Pharisee." Pharisees were the Jewish teachers who believed that Jesus rose from the dead.

The Sadducees believed just as strongly that this never happened. His comment caused a noisy, chaotic, nearly physical fight. The Roman soldiers took Paul away from the scene to protect him. Luke wishes, here, for us to see that these Romans also were believers and that this can be and is acceptable to everyone. Whether Jew, Roman, or Greek, Christianity really is no threat to anyone who matters if the belief is constructive.

Then John's Gospel shows how easy tolerance really is. Jesus had a daily practice of praying. No matter how hard His day was, how tired He really was, He always went off completely by Himself and prayed. Always, His prayer to His father was never for any worldly thing for His own comfort. Instead, He would ask for the blessing of unity upon all who became His followers.

At the request of His followers, Jesus taught them the Lord's Prayer. However, His own prayers were not for forgiveness, daily bread, or freedom from temptation. He prayed for us: all who follow Him and those who will follow Him through the testimony of the Christians who spread the Gospel throughout history.

The model for unity He gives us here is that same unity that exists between the Father and the Son. We saw, in the first reading, how division and disunity tear at the heart of what it means to be a Christian community.

He prays for this unity: "That we will be one united community with one another and with him and with the Father." *(John 17:21)* How different from our own, often, selfish, "Help me with this or let me have that." Often when we do pray for others, it is still only as it relates to ourselves: "Please help me to forgive Bob for being such a jerk."

Unity in Christianity creates unity in the whole world and it starts here with each one of us. Unity is love, justice, and charity.

GOD BLESS YOU.

1 Corinthians 8: 1–7, 11–13; Luke 6: 27–28

✟

What could anyone say that would be more understandable? Saint Luke makes it clear that nothing can be more serious than to cause another, especially an innocent person, to sin.

1 Corinthians uses this example: "Is it sinful to eat flesh that has been sacrificed to idols?" *(1 Corinthians 8:4)* Knowledgeable Christians truly and absolutely refuse to accept idols as something that exists. Therefore, animals offered to idols are offered to nothing; thus, this is perfectly OK as food. There is, though, an occasion in which this freedom does become sinful. Nothing God created is sinful. For us to use it differently from God's intent does make it a sin.

Saint Luke says that Christians must always take into consideration the conscience of others and not scandalize them. Christians do not all have a common belief, though we are closely linked to one another through the community of Christ's body. One person's actions affect the whole community. If my actions scandalize or, in other words, hurt another member, I am not free to do it. Real Christian freedom is the ability to always act responsibly for the common good.

The more authority and honor God gives us, the greater God's expectations of us to avoid creating scandal. The primary audience to whom Jesus spoke these common sense instructions was His disciples and He is radical in His instructions. He does not instruct us to, "Tolerate your enemies," but rather, "Love them." He does not instruct us to , "Refrain from doing harm to those who hate you," but rather, "Do good to them." The key to understanding these "very different" responses is that Jesus is speaking from the perspective of the Kingdom of God. This is a new truth and demands a new way of living.

Jesus strongly advocates giving away personal possessions and the Golden Rule. Living according to ordinary standards of today is not enough. Loving those who love us, doing good to those who do good to us, and lending to those we know can repay us does not qualify as Kingdom-of-God-living.

The criteria Jesus sets for the disciples are to relate and respond to others in the way God responds to them. This is mercy. The Bible shows us how God deals with the poor, the needy, and the persecuted. This is how the disciples are to respond to everyone. God is all loving, all merciful, and all forgiving. So must the disciples of Jesus be. Let me end with a question. Who are the disciples of Jesus?

GOD BLESS YOU.

Micah 5:1–4; Romans 8:28–30; Matthew 1:1–16,18–23

✝

The mother of Jesus is so greatly overshadowed by her son. Today is dedicated to her birth. It occurs nine weeks after her Immaculate Conception day on August 8.

Where, we may ask, did the family go after that day when Jesus was twelve until the wedding feast of Cana some twenty-one years later? We are told in Genesis that He returned home with them and remained obedient.

His father was a carpenter, a builder of fine quality furniture who provided for his family through this profession. That they lived from day to day is quite likely, and they shared with others what they had. And this is the way Jesus wanted His parents to be. He, Himself, was just another boy in town. Joseph and Mary were only a man and woman, just doing what they did best.

Mary was a caring wife, mother, and neighbor. She spent her days doing the needed work in their home. She cared for the home and the needs of her husband and son. Today there are people in the Christian faith who teach that she was a virgin only up until the birth of Jesus. Then she lived as a married woman, giving life to her husband. Some interpret the Bible to mean that she had other children.

The Catholic Church, the church God himself built when Jesus told Simon, "Simon, henceforth you are Peter; upon this rock I will build my church, and the gates of hell will not prevail against it. I give to you the keys to heaven. Whatever you bind on earth will be bound in heaven. Whatsoever you loose on earth is loosed in heaven. Whose sins you forgive are forgiven them. Whose sins you retain are retained," has taught from its beginning that Mary and Joseph both agreed to live celibate lives.

GOD BLESS YOU.

Romans 8:31–39; Luke 13:31–35

✟

The Pharisees, here, warn Jesus not to go into Jerusalem with His teachings. They point out Herod's wish to kill Him. This is very different from their treatment of Him in all the rest of the Bible stories.

Jesus knows exactly what we suspect: They fear Him. His beautiful stories about a loving and forgiving God are grabbing the people's attention.

The Pharisees taught of the same God, but made demanding laws that had to be followed in order for the Israelite people to gain His concern and care. He knew that as He continued toward this large center of their religious activities that those religious leaders would be forced to openly reject Him and show their hypocrisy.

Likewise, the sly untrustworthy "fox" (Herod) would lose followers, who would turn to Jesus because He loves Jerusalem and its people like a Mother Hen who gathers her chicks and protects them. Jesus is God's gift to them and nothing can nor will deter Him from this end.

With this picture of our loving and patient God before us, we must understand that we, too, have a job. It is to sincerely search and uncover the path we must follow, and to face the challenge of moving forward upon this path. We must do it for the right reasons and bring others with us.

Jesus showed us how He did it. First, He dismissed everyone else's advice to stop what He was doing. Second, He ignored Herod's wrath toward Him. Third, He ignored the fears His friends had for His safety, and, fourth, He even dismissed His desire for His own self-preservation. He went directly to Jerusalem because that was God's will for Him.

God, likewise, gives us a lot of liberties, but He never fails to call, in His love and kindness, to bring us back to our destiny to help complete His divine plan and our own deepest desires.

Paul's encouragement to the Romans reminds us, too, that nothing can separate us from God's loving care. We will save ourselves a lot of time and trouble if we simply build the courage to set out in the right direction in the first place.

GOD BLESS YOU.

Wisdom 2: 17–20, James 3: 16–43, Mark 9: 3–37

✝

Giving a homily sends me to read what other people, bright people, have understood about what God says in scripture. Reading the works of others gives me new insights to share with whoever listens.

Today, I have learned that God does not solve our problems because right answers and solutions can only be right if they come from the one who owns the problem. All who have problems must handle them their way, because one's own truths can do it for you, and nobody else's. You can talk to others about them and hope they will only listen.

Back in the days when I did marriage preparations, each couple received a poem titled "When I ask you to listen to me." The first three lines go like this: "When I ask you to listen to me and you start giving advice, you have not done what I asked."

This bit of poetic wisdom tells it like God does it and He shows us how to do it.

Other Gospels mention to turn the other cheek and if someone steals your shirt, give him also your coat. Now, you know, God is not telling you to be a doormat. He is implying much deeper wisdom. I would like you to hear what it is, and to see the common sense in it.

What you earned and need is yours, but before you respond to being misused, just take a look at the thief's life. If he or she is in deep need, reach out to him or her. Help the person find an honest way. Sometimes this takes "tough love," but use it. The reasoning here is that your new friend made a poor choice.

God tells us to not make a second bad one because relations can get nasty. When people rise up beyond smallness, problems get solved. Do listen to the other person because he does have a story to tell.

Political and religious arguments made with strong feelings sometimes get out of hand. If both sides leave the scene angry, nothing has been solved, in fact, more problems get created.

The Pharisees so insisted upon their law that said not to work on the Sabbath that they condemned Jesus for curing a man of his pain and his withered arm. They couldn't understand that sometimes, justice does not mean absolute strict application of the law. Jesus commented, "The Sabbath was made for man, not man for the Sabbath!" *(Mark 2:27)*

For this and other false charges, they had Him killed. But as He quietly accepted the pain and the shame, He won in the end. He rose and went to heaven and His work still goes on far and wide through every one of us.

GOD BLESS YOU.

CHAPTER 3

WISDOM

Life holds a certain sweetness for the humble.
Wise men and women open themselves to God.
They hear his gentle promises, and
Be they wealthy or poor,
Their lives are filled with
Beauty and peace.

Jeremiah 31: 31–34; Matthew 16: 13–23

✟

The prophet Jeremiah prophesied these words: "Jesus will establish a new covenant with the Israelites." *(Jeremiah 31:31)* We know that the word "new" does not always mean brand new, but also carries the meaning "renew." The thought going on here is that rather than being given the Ten Commandments on stone tablets, Jesus will instill His rules directly into our hearts when we open up to Him. This happens when we search for the meanings in His words. It also happens when we read religious materials, listen to stories about His love and forgiveness, we repent, and when we see His helpful hand in these final times filling our hearts with warmth and care.

As He fills our hearts, He fills our way of life and our choices become wholesome. We do things the way He created us to. He leads us to happiness in serving as loving children of His family. Many great men and women in history have spoken out, firmly, because God has given them messages to pass on to the world.

We may wonder how we could gain the courage to pass on His stories. To do this requires true faith and charity. These strengths and this courage come from being open to His graces. God's stories are before us, but are not being heard by many.

Saint John Paul spent his lifetime as Pope, traveling the world over bringing these God stories to young people. Many millions met him with love and admiration. Now, in their adult life, they need to hear from someone that these stories must be passed on by those who heard them from a Saint.

At no time has the world been in greater need of hearing God's words. Lives filled with God are driven to tell His words to others. Each of us are challenged to make them heard in our unique way.

GOD BLESS YOU.

Ezekiel 36: 23–28, Matthew 22: 1–14

✝

The king sent his servants out through the countryside to invite anyone and everyone to his son's wedding feast. Yet, when he discovered a guest inappropriately dressed, he had him thrown outside into darkness.

He had a dress code, like some of our fancy restaurants that require customers to wear a coat and tie or you cannot come in. This sounds ridiculous to me, but Jesus is saying that this is the way heaven is. If you do not meet certain standards, you will be turned away into eternal hell fires. This does not sound like our loving savior, so just what is Jesus trying to say?

Today, we can buy clothes to cover a multitude of undesirable body problems. Fashion magazines have solutions for large hips, broad shoulders, and for bald heads. They want us to look like beautiful gods and goddesses. Now, let me say this: So does our loving Father!

He wants us to look our best on the outside. He also wants us to be beautiful on the inside, to clothe ourselves in His graces, His love, and His goodness. We are to wear the needs for salvation and to mirror the image of Jesus Christ.

If we want to get into God's Heavenly feast we must cover our ugly sin stains with the transforming beauty of Christ, This loving savior is offered to us as the wedding garment, making us a new creation the moment we put it on. We will embrace the makeover by accepting Him fully and do our best to become like Him. The reward is sainthood in heaven.

GOD BLESS YOU.

Jeremiah 18: 1–6, Matthew 13: 47–53
✝

Every faculty we have received from God is a gift making possible our ability to receive God's message of His love for us, His forgiveness, and His path to our peace. His message began with the first man and woman and has run continuously to us today.

In Jeremiah's eighteenth chapter, Jeremiah tells us that he heard these words from God: "Rise up, and be off to the Potter's house." The potter, it is hinted, was God working at the potter's wheel. Symbolically, Jeremiah looked on. God formed the clay to His image. The creation sometimes turned out poorly, but he continued trying, over and over working with the failed clay to make a better object in the way that pleased Him.

All people are molded by His hands, from the dust of the Earth. That is all we are and our bodies return back to that dust when our journey here ends, but we will be raised up, glorified to eternal heaven…or hell's eternal fire, whichever we earned during the time He gave us.

Whenever He has to change our mold, we change, too, and He never gives up on the clay that failed. He is at it till our deathbed.

In Matthew's gospel, many, many times His chosen people of Israel failed to be the way people need to be. He threatened to destroy them as He had done in the great flood and to Sodom and Gomorrah, because there was not one single good, God-loving person there.

However, when the nation of sinners repented, He too, repented his decision and continued His work of remolding His clay figures until they had completed their journey and became angelic for heavenly eternity.

He gave man control over every one of His creations. We have power to plant and to harvest. When our work with them ends, we select the good among what we gather for our use. We discard and destroy whatever fails to meet our expectations. God discards the unworthy people among us into the eternal fires of hell.

It all lies in our own life's choices whether we are received in heaven with all the heavenly bodies or rejected into the fires of hell.

We have only one lifetime to earn our destiny.

GOD BLESS YOU.

Ezekiel 18:25–26; Phillip 2:1–11; Matthew 21:28–32

✝

Previously, as students, we have spent years studying to qualify for college. To be a successful musician we spent many hours practicing. To enjoy playing sports we trained and sacrificed much to become a winning team.

Is God like that? Did He have to practice before He got creation right? Is He building muscles to bring the universe to a conclusion? Is God growing into something more powerful than He is now? Of course not. God is perfect. He cannot grow and He cannot change; that is in His divinity. But, in His incarnation the situation is different.

The Son of God, eternal and equal to the Father in all things, did not hesitate to become human. Remaining divine, He chose to be like us in all things but sin.

Jesus became human, responding to His Father's will in order for us to receive salvation. Like the older son in today's parable, He said yes to his father's request. And like the younger son, Jesus actually went. He became lovingly obedient even accepting crucifixion.

He accepted death and His father bestowed upon Him an exulted name to which every knee on earth, in heaven, and under the earth would bend in honor.

What does this act of obedience that saves our souls say to us? So much took place in His holy family. There is so much for us to see in order to do the greatest job that we are called upon to do.

First of all, Jesus was born a baby who learned by imitating His mother and father. Mary tended His needs with great tenderness and love. He received everything He needed from her and He learned from her to love and be happy with everything God gives.

His father worked hard and provided for the family's needs. Joseph showed Him, first and foremost, to do the best job He can possibly do to bring everyone happiness—to provide that which his talents were meant to do. Joseph and Mary were totally concerned with bringing harmony and happiness to their loved one and to everybody else they served. They did not make a plush living and personal comforts their goal.

Let us note here that their home and their goals brought peace to them.

From their home, like ours, comes forth the energies of higher order in society. Friends, from homes—yours and mine—like theirs, come the basics that make up the world. As the home goes, so goes the world. Like you and me, Jesus came out into the world imitating what He observed at home. (Not so much what He was told, but what He saw going on.) And He carried these habits out to everyone around Him and all who came after Him.

Joseph's and Mary's son was obedient. He respected what God created and loving all people just the way they were, though He didn't hesitate to correct their sinfulness. Jesus left His mark very plainly upon the world because He had a dream to fulfill. He knew what He had to do and He brought us the special strengths that existed in every man and woman who came into his life. Tax collectors and prostitutes changed and became saints because they loved what He offered. They opened their hearts to Him.

It is true, He was divine. It is also true that He was exactly as human as you and me. He grew up to be a man who changed the course of history because His mother and father "showed" Him that peace and prosperity happens when humans honestly work to earn their pay. They provide for the needs of all who depend upon them, and accept the responsibility for everything they do.

Today God implies, "You can and do change the world. Be sure that what you do provides prosperity to as many and as much of

God's creation as you can." It is what you leave behind you when you leave this world that really counts.

Just what are those things we leave behind that can change the world? God tells us in the liturgy of the word.

GOD BLESS YOU.

1 Samuel 4: 11–11, Mark 1: 40–45

✝

We are told today why God uses certain holy persons through whom He works a miracle and why He sometimes chooses not to come to His people's side, but allows them to fail.

In the book of Samuel, the Philistine army defeated the Israelites in one day. Israel then sent to Shiloh and brought up the Ark of the Covenant. The Israelite camp cheered and rejoiced until the Philistines cowered. Israel believed that the Ark's presence would save them, but they lost the war along with thirty thousand soldiers and their enemy took home the Ark. God knew that if He fought for His chosen people, the Ark would become an idol. He chose to let His people lose and to die rather than falsely presume that the presence of the Ark would cause Him to change His intentions.

In my youth, I and many of my friends believed because we were told that wearing a blessed article would protect us from harm. We also believed that number thirteen was unlucky, and that finding a four leaf clover brought good luck.

Saint Christopher's medal hung in many cars. He was supposed to protect you while driving. That did work, but most cars drove under twenty miles per hour! We did keep the Saint Christopher medal in our car and prayed for his protection, and that did border upon idolatry.

Saint Mark tells of Jesus praying over the leper. He is God as well as man. Jesus told the leper plainly and clearly to tell no one but his Priest. He knew that people, upon hearing this, would think Him to be a miracle healer only, not as a teacher of God's will and ways, which He was.

Those of us who get excited about blessed men and women of our own day have seen miraculous healing happen to people after praying, namely Blessed John Paul and the Blessed Kateri Tekakwitha. They are mediums God uses to heal.

The point in all this is that God loves us. He does not want us to place high values upon valueless things. In His love, He wants us to seek success through our own abilities to bring the world happiness.

All His stories point to His presence to provide the energy to get us where we need to go. But—we succeed only when we provide the effort. All His stories make us more knowledgeable of His presence and we more clearly understand His gifts and that we are just a little below the angels. We are capable of filling up His world with love for all creatures and creations.

GOD BLESS YOU.

Wisdom 1:13–15, 2:23–24
✝

On the July 4, we in the United Stated celebrate more than two hundred years of independence. Because it happened so long ago, much of the hype and excitement has changed, but the occasion is remembered.

Such changing parallels happen within all matter of our world. Earthly things rise to a peak, and then begin to dwindle and life changes. Along with change, need arises and must be alive for health to grow.

A healthy world requires that we don't forget our past, good or bad. We need knowledge of the past to build our present and future. Wise people, called sages by writers of history, continue to tell the stories about patriotic people whose sacrifices have created a safe environment for the people of their times, as well as for the multitudes that follow. So we must not forget how they offset evils from the past.

This is the wisdom of ages. It must be listened to and digested.

Wisdom stories relate life within the will and designs of God who created it all. Though we have no direct answers to His will and His ways, we accept the mysteries and all is OK. Simply put, wisdom deals with life and death and the presence of good and evil in our world.

Everyone learns how to live comfortably with differences and change. God's love creates and builds up; destruction comes through evil. Often, the question is asked, "If God is so good, why is there injustice and suffering?" The book of Wisdom states that all God created is good and that He also totally respects human freedom. In freedom, painful things occur and some people choose to be unjust. This creates the tensions and sorrows.

So where is God? Right here among us. We just need to turn to Him until our problems get solved. It is important for us to remember that all situations change and all things end. Through His divine love he allows the world freedom to change at its own pace. As this all happens, the wise turn to Him when matters go beyond their ability to handle.

Last week we saw that Jesus calmed the winds and the waves when His disciples came to Him in their desperate fears. In today's gospel two persons came to Him with similar fears and needs. Jarius's little girl was dying. On their way to Jarius's house, an ill woman, desperate for healing, reached out to touch His clothing.

Before He reached the home of the little girl, news came that she had died, but he continued His walk. Amid jeers, He moved through the crowd, along with some apostles and the little girl's mother and father. Death had become the tension for His loving, calming touch. He reached out, took the child's hand in his. She was healed.

Jesus is lord of all creation and creation continues to live freely as He intends it. This makes life real. He loves everybody and everything just the way He finds them and loves them enough to call them forward beyond the way He found them, thus offering Himself as example. Thus, Jesus is perfect. He is not a spectacle meant to astound us, but a healing place for us to turn. He accepts us with all our shortcomings, allows us to live as we choose, and He heals with His touch when we turn to Him.

He is a map for us on our journey to perfection.

GOD BLESS YOU.

Malachi 3:13–20, Luke 11:5–13
☩

Many people go back to gambling machines, feeding them quarter after quarter, sometimes spending $100 or more. Occasionally they get a return. Yet they keep going back and repeat feeding their quarters into the devouring machine. Their driving force is the excitement over the possibility of scoring a huge pot and becoming wealthy by the lucky pull of the handle. We know the odds of that are next to impossible.

What we don't even have any inkling about, however, is just what happens when a normal wage earner or poor person suddenly becomes very wealthy. Among my acquaintances have been some who've inherited large sums. Their lives slipped out of control and they spent all their money. In less unfortunate cases, they bought many comforts, but neglected family and friends, developed superiority attitudes, and lost their ability to care.

At any rate, their lives changed rapidly and changes that got ahead of humility and common sense turned into downhill slides leading to disgust and sometimes depression. How many, on the other hand, lose their faith and all their trust in God when the evils of life strike a blow, leaving them hurting?

Some lose faith in God. They fail to see any other point of view except, "Where is God? How can He sit by and allow such horrible things happen?"

Unfortunately, men and women keep gambling, hoping for a chance they'll get wealthy.

All these desires are for perishable outcomes, but it seems we do not trust the God that Jesus envisions in our gospel. That God is one who knows what we need and one who would never let us down. We know what is good for our children. How much more does God know what is good for us?

Instead of gambling, take time to ask Him for what we desire, which allows us to focus on the God who gives. God will respond, but it may take some time. Jesus uses the image of persistence as a virtue that can wear down the man in the story. We do not wear God down, but we must be persistent and clear about what we want. We can be assured that God will grant us what we need in a lot less time than it will take for the lottery to pay off.

The Holy Spirit is the ultimate gift. What we really want that will benefit us most "is" God's gift. Hang in there. The pay-off is incredible!

While the allurements of the world shall pass away, whoever does God's will shall live forever.

GOD BLESS YOU.

Ezekiel 36:23–28, Matthew 22:1–14
✝

Jesus tells us a story to help us see more deeply the way the hand of God never stops working to help us find truth. We, by working so that others get what they need, create harmony in life.

Giving to others is even more rewarding than receiving.

To get our attention, Jesus exaggerates the hand of Satan at work in our hearts. In this, He shows how our venial sins lead to major ones.

In His story, a king invites his chosen people to his son's wedding feast, which he very elaborately prepares so they may find joy and can relax in the finest settings and company.

You heard, in the parable, their stubborn rejection to their loving lord's invitations. Some chose to stay home and work; some beat—and even killed—those servants who came to remind them to prepare properly and come to His beautiful place of happiness.

Then in anger, the king annihilated those guests on his list who mistreated his servants. After abolishing them, he ordered that all people be invited from wherever they can be found so that the banquet would not be wasted. Here lies a golden egg.

Each of us can recall the times that we, too, have rejected God's messengers He sent to remind us of our faults. Many came forward. They filled the banquet hall and they ate and drank the best prepared food and the finest wine.

But one person here stands out. He probably came right from his job. He didn't take time to cleanse himself nor to change out of his dirty clothes. Smelling with the odors of his job, this fellow must have been offensive to the rest who carefully prepared themselves.

Those working poor who enjoyed the magnificent beauty of the king's palace feast probably asked him over and over to go home and get cleaned up. He made no effort and word of his ill preparation got back to the king.

We heard what happened. How sad, how helpless, even how angry this man must have felt. He had seen the beautiful place with all its color, comforts, and happy people, and then was bound and thrown helplessly out into the cold and dark where he could still hear the laughter and strains of jolly music.

He was near to the celebration with wonderful people, and then lost all only because he simply refused to clean himself and become pleasing to those who had. He was denied all only because he came unprepared before the face of his lord.

Jesus told stories because within them we can see ourselves, and when we discover His lesson, we can find ways to make ourselves worthy.

Let's look closely at our intentions. Pleasing others is the basis for our own beauty and joy. God loves you and is always speaking to you in all possible ways. Please listen.

GOD BLESS YOU.

Ecclesiastes 1:2–11, Luke 9:7–9

✝

This story is the beginning lines of Ecclesiastes, also known as the Book of Qoheleth. It does not inspire happiness, but rather calls our attention to what humans see and do with all the beautiful things our loving Father sends for us.

Let us first look at one of the lesser of these blessings: the few weeks of ultimate beauty of the colorful autumn lying ahead of us. Qoheleth says this is all just vanity. Do we flourish in great joy over it? Or, do we live in mediocre pleasure by looking past its beauty and being remorseful at the season that follows?

In honesty, we do need to agree with Qoheleth. He looked at humans and saw our nature, our emotions, and responses have never changed. He looked at history and saw it repeats itself: What people see and hear does not satisfy them. And he has observed that time erases memory of what has gone on before.

Humans tend to not learn from past mistakes. Wars follow wars. Corruption infects governments…and…even churches. Advertising corrupts our senses. The Herods of our own day work against the common good. Elections create hopes that are often dashed when the elected people take office.

Should Christians read the book of Ecclesiastes?

It can help us face life honestly and look at where man has come from, and realistically, where we are today. It can help us envision what Christ has given us and where we have gone with it. It can prod us to examine our own consciences to see how we might be making the world a more difficult place to live in.

This book can, in the words of Psalm 90, "Teach us to recount our days correctly, that we may gain wisdom of heart."

GOD BLESS YOU.

Philippians 3: 3–8, Luke 15:1–10

✝

In his letter to the Philippians, Paul admits to having been a "lost sheep" from God's flock. For a number of years, he saw himself as the hero, a man of power, a success. He was a wealthy Pharisee who far outdid everyone in killing those who followed Christ. A lost sheep he was, until God carried him into His loving Christian fold. Today, Paul is one of God's greatest saints. In his letter, he looked back and compared himself to the way he was then and the way he was when he wrote the letter.

He understood the evils of his former, worldly glorified self and his new, just, life - filled with peace - within the limits God has given

Today's letter he wrote while he was a prisoner chained to the wall of a Roman dungeon. His joy and peace never "dwindled" because they came from God's promised graces that help withstand the most torturous treatment life can hand out.

There is, yet, even a much deeper glorious story in Paul's letter: Sometimes "I" am that lost sheep. I get worried about what people think of me. Selfishly, I get caught up in fear over being too generous with my time and money and I want to withdraw rather than reach out to do what is right by Christian standards and those God calls for. Sometimes, I get angry because I think someone is trying to change me through his or her words, or I think he or she seems to feel they are superior to me. I think the person feels I am inferior. During these feelings, I choose to look for the other person's flaws and dwell upon them to make myself feel better. I fail to choose to hear God's words: "Son, I always love you. You have so many beautiful, constructive talents. Please, put them forward to benefit the world."

During those times when I am being a lost sheep, it becomes so easy to look at someone else's faults rather than looking at my own. Really, I am a pretty darn good person overall…just like

---

everyone else...most of the time. It is when I allow myself to make excuses, feel righteous, and feel better than someone else that I am a lost sheep and wandering.

Saint John Paul said in his biography, "A saint is one who, more and more gives up his/her attachment to the world and accepts poverty. A true saint finds God in everybody and everything." *(Witness to Hope: The Biography of Pope John Paul II, by George Weigel, HarperCollins Publishers, 2005)*

Once we start looking for God in all these things, we will find Him there. We will no longer be lost. If we wander off again, we will find our way back, and like Paul, will feel joy in what we do have.

GOD BLESS YOU.

CHAPTER 4

FORGIVENESS

*As new stories come to life for you and me, may
we discover new powers in ourselves. May we
realize the powerful effect our words and
actions have upon those lives we touch.*

*And may we become aware that,
even without trying,
we are vessels bringing awareness of God
to vast numbers of nonbelievers.*

2 Corinthians 11:1–11, Matthew 6:7–17

✟

This is the second time the church has presented the Lord's Prayer as our gospel. Clearly its message is what the church wants us to hear and use to form our lives. Many of us learned the prayer as a child at our mother's knee when the meaning of the words were not fully grasped. Now, today, when we hear "Our Father who art in Heaven," we often still mouth the familiar words, but with our minds wandering elsewhere.

Despite the words we're saying, often in our hearts we are really not asking God to do anything. "Ask" is the correct word here. In the New Testament, the word "pray" almost always means "ask." Prayer is not just a pious act; it is a request. When Jesus said, "This is how you are to pray," the words might be better translated as, "This is how you are to ask God for *your needs.*"

So it makes good sense that Matthew introduces the Lord's Prayer by quoting Jesus' words about what *not* to ask for, like fine food, beautiful clothing, and exotic shelter. In faith, God knows our needs and has provided a world that, if we tend it right and help one another, meets those needs. Jesus says to ask God to do what only God can do—bring about His kingdom of Heaven now, to our world—a kingdom characterized by peace and forgiveness.

God freely extends forgiveness to us, but we have to cooperate with that gift. The church's mission is to extend that forgiveness to everyone—the entire people of God. John the Baptist describes Jesus as the Lamb of God who takes away the sins of the world. Jesus' final words to His disciples on Easter were, "As the Father has sent me, so I also send you. Whose sins you forgive are forgiven them"…God's life in us, His church, is what enables us to do that. This is His kingdom, which we are to continue to ask for.

A young Jewish girl had the horrible experience in World War II of watching her sister being beaten to death by a German guard in a

---

concentration camp. She escaped and returned some years later to give a talk in Germany. A man came up to thank her for her presentation and extended his hand. As she looked into his face, to her horror, she recognized him as the one-time German soldier who had savagely killed her sister. She froze and could not bring her hand up to shake his.

She cried out silently, "Jesus, help me!" Slowly her hand came up and clasped his. He, seeing the turmoil in her face recognized immediately what was going on. He fell to his knees, weeping and begging her forgiveness, which she had given when she accepted his hand. She had been enabled to give him not only her forgiveness, but also God's.

Saint Francis DeSales says, "We cannot always offer God great things, but each instant we can offer him little things in big ways."

GOD BLESS YOU.

Genesis 44: 18–21, 23–29; 45: 1–5; Matthew 10: 7–15

✝

Yesterday we heard the story of the politically powerful Joseph. God moved him into this place of prestige for the good of the world.

The Bible contains some stories that are refreshing and quite exciting. From the book of Genesis_we have such an appealing one today—at least for me. One of my favorite themes deals with human hurts brought on by acts of envy by one who loves the victim, but who forgets that love or hatred both exist and are choices. As today's story unfolds, the guilty get introduced to true God-given love of a brother for brother. They quietly repent their angry feelings, ask forgiveness, give and receive genuine love, and all becomes well.

Beautiful things happened when Brother Judah begged to take the punishment for his young brother, Benjamin. His father had suffered greatly when Joseph disappeared, and would suffer to death if his youngest son, Benjamin, were to be imprisoned. As Judah pleaded, Joseph dismissed everyone who was not family then tearfully told them, "I am your brother, Joseph." The scene became filled with awe, tears, and joy as these strong and harsh men emotionally received their brother's forgiveness.

There is much more to this story. Like all stories of the Bible, for lack of time and space, much gets left out. We are not told what went on inside Joseph's heart. Sold into slavery, he must have had, as all humans would, some anger against his jealous brothers. Taken from the security of his home and forced to perform the servile work of a slave, he must've had feelings of homesickness.

However, inside himself he had convictions, learned at home that whatever he felt, whatever he did, these were choices he would make. As he slaved, his feelings and actions must have caught favorable attention from the other workers, as the men who supervised him, because when Pharaoh sought help and found none from his wise men about the meaning of his dream, the slave, Joseph, was recommended. He correctly interpreted Pharaoh's dream to mean there would be seven years of plenty followed by seven years of famine. He was made ruler over the collection and distribution of food, which saved the entire world.

He realized when his brothers came and knelt before him that all the pain in his life had been taken by God and made into a thing of beauty. He was the salvation of the tribe of Jacob and of the whole world. He changed. He dismissed his anger over his unjust brothers' act. He gave up his desire for revenge, forgave, and was rewarded with genuine love. He returned to father and family.

Because of his brothers' sinful jealousy and his suffering, God's will for the Israelites was fulfilled.

God also assures us through this story that He will accept and forgive all our sins, and use our weaknesses to fulfill His divine will. But one more message lies here: One among us, the least among us, just might be His vessel and save the world. Through your sorrows, your pains, your fears, God will lead many to salvation.

GOD BLESS YOU.

Ezekiel 12:1–12, Matthew 18: 21–29

✛

Matthew's Gospel is an interesting story that teaches why Jesus so strongly stresses forgiveness. He uses an exaggerated example to impress upon us that it is not about the number of times or about the degree of the hurt, but that forgiveness is a "must" and people have to be forgiven. Peter offered the number seven because in the scriptures, seven symbolizes the number of perfection.

God worked six days creating earth and sky and seas. The seventh He made holy (perfect) by resting and looking back fondly upon what He had done. However, Jesus called for seventy-seven times, symbolizing endless forgiving.

Why is forgiveness such a must? First of all, we tell God in the Lord's Prayer, "If I do not forgive others, do not forgive me." Secondly and far better, "I forgive because I have been forgiven much." Let's look at an example of this case: How many people attend Mass on Sunday because not doing so without good reason is a serious sin? Compare this to, "I attend to offer thanks for all my graces and gifts." In this same vein, forgiveness of others is an opportunity to live in peace and love. Mental health professionals caution that emotional healing demands letting go of anger.

I once worked for a man with low self-image. Because of this, he did many things to intimidate me and force me to feel inferior to himself. He succeeded and I became depressed. Later, I joined the twelve-step program that alcoholics use. My life reopened when I was instructed to write a list of everyone I needed to forgive. My discovered secret was that I was filled with suppressed anger. Healing took a long time. Through prayer, sympathy from my wife, Barb, and a few other trustworthy friends, I grew. I found love again, and again I could smile from my heart.

In the Prodigal Son story, we feel the great joy of the Father when his son came home to him. He never stopped loving him and waiting prayerfully for his return.

In confession, too, we feel God's joy when we have sorrow for even our most venial sin.

We are in dire need of God's help to repent, but to hear the priest's words, "I forgive you," lifts a load from one's heart.

Hurts must be forgotten. Love will replace them.

GOD BLESS YOU.

Corinthians 8: 1–7, 11–13, Luke 6:27–38

✝

We are challenged in these words from Jesus today to do one of the most difficult tasks in life. He says "Love your enemies, do good to those who hate you, bless those who curse you, pray for the person who mistreats you." Christ continues with other behaviors: When physically attacked or when someone steals what is yours, He tells us how we should respond. Further, one is not to judge or condemn, but should focus on forgiving and giving.

Even as wonderful as our United States is, as well as many foreign lands, we see pettiness. We see power and control and authority used to "get even" with others, even though we live in Christian lands.

The August 23, 2012 *Omaha World Herald* newspaper carried an article, a report, that fifty-two women and children were killed in Kenya. A local official said, "The killings were revenge attacks after a string of cattle thefts." On August 26 of this year, television reported 440 Syrian people killed. The claim was revenge killings of civilians who had supported government rebels. We likely will not encounter these extremes. However, many other negative behaviors happen.

God calls us to, "Love your enemy, bless those who curse you, pray for the person who mistreats you."

Our world needs to be shown this. In a gospel that we will hear soon, we are shown Jesus teaching His apostles that the Son of God will be shamed, tortured, and die. In this same scene, Peter takes Him aside and says, "I will not allow this to happen to you. I will get up a group of men, some who will be willing to die protecting you!"

Imagine, for a few seconds, how the human Jesus was pleased with this thought. But instantly He recognized that Satan was also

---

in this. Then, before He could entertain these thoughts, it came to Him that the main reason He had come down from heaven was to suffer. Immediately, He cast the devil out, saying, "Get behind me, Satan!" Then to himself as well as to the big fisherman He said, "You are thinking not as God thinks, but as man does!" In these scriptures, God shows us not only how to resist the devil and his temptations, but also **why**.

Even more beautifully, He has chosen you today, and me, to hear and see these scenarios. He is saying, "You are special! I love you! I trust you! I am calling you to show the world how to resist temptations from hell and to replace them in this world with smiles and kindness, prayer, and love!" This brings the kingdom to earth.

GOD BLESS YOU.

CHAPTER 5

FAITH

Life is a beautiful gift!
How I choose to handle things that happen is what
I give to the world.
The world grows stronger or becomes weaker from the way I feel and react to Its offerings.
It takes…FAITH.

Job 3:1–3, 11–19. 20–23; Luke 9:51–56

✝

Written between the years 500–700 BC, the book of Job is one of the most beautifully written pieces of literature. It is ranked among the top literary masterpieces of all times. It is poetry, and to see the beauty of poetry, it is necessary to note the images carried in each line, even in each word.

Job is an oriental chieftain, very God-loving, upright, and extremely wealthy. But you know his horrible fate. Reading closely, we can see his innocent total deprivation, which parallels that of our redeemer.

As this narrative flows along, it shows that the suffering of innocents, those who do not lose faith, are relieved by the hand of God. As He brings the solution, the rewards exceed what they had been given in their lives before.

Job trusted God throughout it all. He rejected his old friends, who insisted that somewhere something in his ways had offended God deeply. However, he remained true and kept his faith.

See here, first of all, that, even the most innocent suffer. Their suffering is the test of fidelity. This trust must never be lost. This trust will bring the sufferers through to greater reward than was ever the case before.

Our minds cannot even fathom the depth of God's divine knowledge and care.

Luke's Gospel shows Jesus, rejected by a Samaritan village, responding to rejection with a calm disposition. He scolded His disciples for getting upset and for wanting to destroy those bigots. In peace, they moved on to another town for their nights, and to receive food and peaceful sleep.

A calm and untroubled life can be ours, also, when we accept antagonizing situations and face our problems, aware of God's power and mercy, His presence, and His wisdom.

Problems get solved when we react to dishonor with honor.

GOD BLESS YOU.

1 Corinthians 12:12–14, 27–31; Luke 7: 11–17

✝

Paul and Luke combine to create this picture of what the original Christian church was like. Then, as now, it was a healthy, growing, human affair. They who became and remained disciples accepted the knowledge that all form one body and that each person is a genuine part whose efforts make it work.

Each person has unique gifts that combine to form a single group with a single end.

Paul cautions that, yes, the members are widely different, but by looking at how similar we are, it all comes together. When we reach for the final goal, the gift of charity with love is the glue. Love puts all the gifts from all the factions at the service of the community.

Saint Luke shows how Jesus is the ultimate of charity, with His love the glue.

The cultures of Rome and Greece were patriarchal. Males stood at the head of all in their society. Women worked for their husbands, to help them carry their efforts to fulfillment. Unfortunately, though, if a woman's husband died, she could only survive by begging unless she was fortunate enough to have a son or to remarry.

Today, most women rightfully hold high, respectable places in society and the stigma is subsiding. The message today is this: As the body of Christ, we are to give equality to all from our personal gifts so that all who work together are equal; all are responsible parts.

Jesus is the core. He takes the feeblest people and creates many beautiful results through our very concern and care.

GOD BLESS YOU.

1 Corinthians 6:1–12, Luke 6: 12–19

✟

Saint Paul tells the Corinthians to have their differences settled by church people, godly men. Selfishly, they sue one another in Roman courts using pagan attorneys.

God's mystifying ways are shown here as different from the ways of man. God made no two people alike. Each person differs in temperament and talents. It is through our differences we are able to complete His work.

Jesus promised that all would come into one flock. This will happen, but to look to the Holy Lands around Jerusalem today is despairing. The three major religions, each with its own understanding of God's truths, stand at great odds with one another. Yet we all contribute to his cause and He promises we will all come together into a single flock.

The prophet Jeremiah, in his letter to the Israelites when they were captives in Babylon, tells what God promises: "I will restore the tents of Jacob. His city shall be rebuilt upon the hill. From them will resound songs of praise and laughter of happy people. I will punish oppressors and you shall be my people; I will be your God."

God promises that He will take everything we do, be it tiny and simple, or be it large and significant, and He will gather it all into a harmonious whole.

There is absolutely no need for us to despair. Just trust, believe, and be thankful for life and all He gives. As we learn to accept what comes along, let us never forget that through God, everything and everybody will become good. He only asks that we do something with our talents and possessions. Live life charitably and He will put it together for the good of the world.

Jeremiah writes God's words during Israel's captivity, a time of great despair and depression, when he says, "With age old love, I have loved you. I will restore you. You shall be rebuilt—O- Virgin, Israel. You shall again go forth dancing. You shall again plant vineyards and enjoy the fruit."

In our world today, people who gossip about people hurting people just do not get God's way.

God will take it all under His power. The poor in spirit will rejoice in laughter. He will send away their persecutors empty.

God exists in each of us in the good that is there. Through us He will bring all to completion in His divine love.

GOD BLESS YOU.

Colossians 1: 9–14; Luke 5:1–11

✝

Today, Jesus chose for us here to see much further beyond our shallow, human insights. In the Gospel story, His apostles had fished all night. They dragged the deep, the shallows, and those places where they had success before, but caught nothing.

Tired from their strenuous work through the entire hot humid night, they are now cleaning up to hang the nets to dry until another day, expecting now to rest and relax. Jesus changed their plans.

Jesus was surrounded by a large crowd of Jews from all walks of life who were pressing to hear his story about heaven, justice, and peace. He finally had to get into Simon's boat. A few yards out from shore, Jesus preached and His listeners wanted more. When He ended, He instructed His big fisherman apostle to try fishing again. With reluctance, Simon did as his Lord instructed and we know what happened.

By now our minds should be rolling around the Spiritual implications that Luke's scenario is playing out. A very great feeling of satisfaction lies in seeing the great hunger in the hearts of these people as Jesus makes it known that they are loved by their all-complete God who first created the beauty-filled world, and then put them in it to find happiness and work for eternal and complete love in heaven.

GOD BLESS YOU.

Daniel 7: 9–10, 13–14; (Rev. 12:7–12); John 1:47–51

☦

Genesis chapter 32 relates to us the story of the Jew, Jacob. He had a dream. He saw angels going up and down a ladder to and from heaven, and a short time later, wrestled with God's representative, injuring his hip. Here he was given the name "Israel," which means "one who strives with God." His house and all his descendants became God's chosen people about whom the Exodus story tells.

Another implication exists here. This strange occurrence has a powerful message for us, to see influences of God's Holy Spirit working in our lives. Sin stalks us with temptations of immediate pleasure. Because we know God's wishes, a spiritual battle takes place for us. When we persist in righteousness and do not give in, especially when the desire to sin seems overwhelming, we come through it like the Israelites, as God's chosen sons and daughters did. And when the struggle is over and heaven breaks through, we end up much closer to Jesus and much more like Him.

Our help from heaven on Earth is God's angels. Today we celebrate the three archangels. We are familiar with Michael, who drove Satan out of heaven down to Hell. Saint Gabriel was the angel who gave Mary her great message, and Raphael is known as God's healer. God sends him to bring healing to those who ail.

The Holy Catholic Church teaches that heaven and Earth are filled with angels whose spirits surround us and come to us when we are challenged.

Most of my young life, every morning and evening, my mother had me and my siblings kneel at her lap and say our prayers. We always ended with the words, "Angel of God, my guardian dear, God's love for me has sent you here," and you all know the rest of the prayer to our guardian angel. This continued through most of my life: kneeling down at the side of my bed and meditating upon these prayers. I had been taught that from among this multitude of spiritual beings, one was assigned to be by my side, guide me from tragic harm, and to lead me out of temptation. This angel is another gift from God to aid me through my earthly journey.

So much is written, discussed, and preached about God and his saints and angels, and during our lifetime we only absorb a smidgeon of that knowledge about them. Holy Mother Church wants to help us become as complete spiritually as we can be. It behooves us, then, to recognize the places where God sends His angels to touch our lives. Also, there is great peace when these spirits feel close at hand.

GOD BLESS YOU.

Maccabees 2:15–19, Luke 19:41–49

✝

Jesus assured mankind that day when He said, in effect, these words to Simon, "You are the rock upon whom I will build my church—which will defeat hell!"

Today in the readings, Maccabees and Luke send our minds back to these hopeful, inspiring words, especially amid worldly turmoil and anti-God movements. People of the world, we come to understand as we become more knowledgeable, have never ever been different.

Our readings are from an early time in God's prophetic years when Antiochus, who was once a hostage in Rome, came to power in Greece. During his reign, there arose among the Israelites unhappy men who turned to the gentiles and began to worship their idols.

They took a plan to Antiochus to force all people to honor their idol gods and he promoted them.

When these idols were brought to Modein, they met Mattathias and offered him wealth, power, and nobility if he knelt to the altar of idols. His response was, "I, my sons, and my kinsmen will keep the covenant of our father. God forbid that we should forsake the laws and commandments." Then an Israelite came forward to make his offering at the altar of Modein. Mattathias, in his great zeal for faith, sprang up and killed him, along with the king's messengers.

He then walked through the town calling to all to refuse idol worship and follow him. Many heard, abandoned all they owned, and went up with him into the mountains. Many others went another way. Taking their cattle and possessions, they moved out into the desert.

These people were later slain by Antiochus's army. The Bible tells us that they put forth no resistance. They moved forward, faced the slayers, and accepted death over abomination. Such incidents happened in the New Testament.

Mattathias, on the other hand, was followed into the mountains by a group called Hesidians, valiant Israelites, and all devoted followers of Jewish law. They formed a strong army, led by Mattathias, and slew sinners, those who broke the law, when they fled to Roman gentiles for protection. This army went about destroying Pagan altars. They put to flight the arrogant and subdued all the power of hell.

For us, what a reassuring story this is, even to this day. God gives us all we need to dispel hell's fury. God gave the church you…and me. He teaches through His priests that in peace, charity, and love we can help conquer all of hell. He gives us all that we need.

GOD BLESS YOU.

Job 19: 21–27, Luke 10:1–12

✝

Our stories from Job and Luke's Gospel both show love surviving through harshness and pain, and how love turns that pain into joy.

A very wealthy, faithful, and contented Job suddenly lost everybody he most dearly loved and everything he owned. Adding to his misery, all of his valued friends continuously derided him, telling him to admit his grave sin and repent.

In face of this all, he never lost sight of what was true: that he had never sinned, and that God is a loving God and will in His time mercifully restore His happy and rich life. He knows that God is love and that He allows total freedom to man and nature. He is ever beside us, offering graces to get us through the worst the world can give.

In Luke's Gospel, Jesus sends out over seventy disciples to tell the story of God, and as he put it, like lambs among wolves, they are to take along absolutely nothing for their comforts or their hygiene. He told them to walk into their cities, wish the people peace, and where they are welcomed, stay the entire time accepting only what their host sets before them.

Job knew and stood by the comfort that he never sinned, that God is just and will make all things come to right. This faith carried him through his lengthy time of trouble.

The seventy three went forward exactly as instructed and spread the good news and were fulfilled. Some were given much, some received very limited hospitality, and some were rejected. These, in turn, rejected those cities and moved on.

The end result is this: We see that God is always beside us to get us through. What happens to us in the middle of a crisis is our own choice. We can dote upon bad luck or we can continue to

----

trust God, accept the pain, and know it will end. Meanwhile, be grateful to God, whose graces give us strength we need to be patient. It takes no more energy to be positive than it does to be negative.

Life gets far more rewarding for us who love our neighbors, play down our own pain, and seek to raise the level of happiness for everyone God sends to us. This "giving" builds the peace the entire world needs.

Your power of one is limitless.

GOD BLESS YOU.

CHAPTER 6

HUMILITY AND TRUST

Enjoy the little things God has set around you.

Take on your obligations;

solve them while they are small.

Then the world will be yours, and so will everything that's in it. And you will be happy, pleased, and at peace. This is God's promise!

Esther 12:14:16:23–25; Matthew 7:7–12

✝

Speaking to you and to me personally today in the Bible, God tells us that His part in a relationship with us is constant, but His is the smaller part. If a relationship is to exist, we have to slow down the outside noises. If we wish to be at peace, we must listen to His voice, which comes to us as subtle thoughts. That is Him!

This all came out in Esther's story, in her deep, fear-filled problem. Esther was an extremely beautiful Jewish girl. King Ahasuerus, not knowing her ancestry, made her his wife and queen of his domain.

In the story, Haman, a high-ranking person among the king's men, hated Jews. He had a plan to obtain the king's permission to kill them all. (Not just a present-day problem in the world.)

Mordecai, the Jewish leader at that time, learned about Haman and his heinous plan. He went before Queen Esther and told her that she was the only chance to sway the King to refuse this senseless slaughter of innocent men, women, and children.

Now Esther became very deeply afraid. She would, first of all, have to reveal her ancestry. The Jews, as conquered people, were only to be slaves. Her husband customarily became totally angry. She stood to be shamefully and painfully put to death, Mordecai publicly hanged, and every living Jew killed.

Matthew, in his Gospel, tells us what God advises every person to do when life gives out seemingly impossible problems: "Ask and it will be given you. Seek and you will find. Knock and the door will be opened to you." To all who do so, it will be granted! "Do unto others what you would have them do unto you."

This poor, frightened young girl had the world lying upon her shoulders and she raised her eyes to God. She did a great

---

penance. Setting aside her rich finery, she wrapped herself in the humbling garb of grieving, gunny sacks. She sat upon an ash pile, sprinkling the ashes over her body until her beauty became detestable. Then she asked! She asked God to stand beside her because she was going before her husband and beg for the lives of the Jews.

Esther then cleaned herself and again put on her queenly finery. Her great beauty shone and then fearfully she went before the king. She prostrated herself. How we wish her success as we read her story!

God opened the door! King Ahasuerus, looking upon his queen's exquisite beauty and seeing her deep humility, told her, "Ask anything even half of my kingdom and I will grant it."

She told him about his man, Haman, and his plan to exterminate her people. She explained that Haman had built a formidable hanging scaffold in the public square to kill Mordecai, and then he planned to exterminate her and all her people.

As expected, the king grew totally angry and stormed out. That sleepless night, dwelling upon his anger, he ordered that Haman be brought to his self-built scaffold and publicly hanged. His God-loving, humble wife he placed upon a second throne right beside his from where she could reign alongside whenever she chose.

Ask and it will be given to you! Seek and you will find! Knock and the door will be opened to you, along with much more. Loving people who know God, as we see in this story, knock, seek, and ask in true humility, and they find true peace in their troubles. God answers "Yes" to their requests.

GOD BLESS YOU.

Genesis 17:3–9, John 8:51–59

✞

I grew up on a farm. Life was simple and people trusted people. My father bought his seed for the fields, paid for as much seed as there was money for, and the elevator owner knew that he would get the rest in the fall after harvest. Both lived happy on less. Interest was not tacked on, but agreeable compensation was offered.

This trust, we are shown here, reaches all the way back to earliest man. It happened among the humble and between people who needed one another. This trust got lost when people became independently wealthy and able to buy the things they needed as they needed them.

The point here is that everything in creation changes, and along with change comes a lot of good. Also comes some unfortunate matters, and everyone has to accept both and go on with life.

We see here before us, in the Old Testament, this type of trust existed between God and people. Our gospel tells us that Abram is directed by God to leave his homeland and to move to a distant place. He takes his wife and his brother and they drive their livestock to the land God had for them.

Ninety-plus years old and childless, Abram, with his aged wife, Sarah, far past childbearing years, were promised, in God's words, "Then I will make your descendants as numerous as the sands on the shore. I will be their God! They will be my people." *(Genesis 17:3-9)* Abram trusted God's promise and went to this unknown land and new life, trusting that all was going to be fine, as he was promised. They were blessed. God gave them a baby, Isaac. We know some of his story. From him, God's promise of many descendants came about. It all happened because of a grace-filled husband and wife. They trusted God's Word.

Today, we've also been promised, "Whoever keeps my word will never taste death." *(John 8:51)* We do trust, do give Him glory, and accept all that happens in life.

The wise among us know that eternity exists. We are promised joy far beyond what we have. He will give without end.

He gives His heavenly love, peace, and wisdom. He will share with us without even a handshake, just upon His word. It will happen. Trust!

GOD BLESS YOU.

2 Kings 24: 8–17, Matthew 7: 21–29

✝

The book of Kings differs from most other books in the Bible. It is historical. It doesn't provide excitement to me because the people and places are completely different than those I have visualized. But people of God know that He uses any and all means to reveal Himself. Jehoiachin's short reign here teaches that he and others were spiritual, practical, cop outs. They chose to use their wealth and power for their own pleasures. They delved into the world of luxury and sin. This story shows that their rejection of Yahweh and their Torah became the move toward Judah's downfall. This sounds a bit familiar. God is patient. If He has even a small number of followers, He sends His prophets and waits for repentance. When repentance fails to occur, He allows His free, sinning people to get beaten down.

After Babylon's victory over Judah, all significant able people were made slaves, and all wealth and valuables were taken to sinful Babylon. However, as this story progresses, the Israelites begin to reform and then repent. God then sent good men to lead them back to His land of milk and honey. Just going to church or saying prayers, we are told here, does not guarantee salvation. We are also called to reverent communication, loving ways, and obedience to His commands. Jesus said earlier, "I did not come to abolish the law." *(Matthew 5:17)*

The history of our ancestors in the Old Testament shows again and again kingdoms falling back into paganism.

When they shut out Yahweh, they cut themselves off from the source of their power and secure future.

When our country was young, our country's founders struggled to get the thirteen colonies to come into the new national union. Benjamin Franklin addressed the members of parliament, indicating we need to pray. He pushed that God helped us when

---

we were fighting for independence and we needed his help forming the union. He suggested that every meeting should begin with prayer. This didn't happen, but his words helped calm them so that the business of founding the federal government went forward.

Jesus stresses the importance of building upon rock, not sand.

Today our nation, our church, and our very selves are called to review the sincerity of our commitment to God. Token prayers are insufficient. Our words and our actions must solidly demonstrate what our money affirms, "In God we trust."

GOD BLESS YOU.

Ecclesiastes 1:2–11, Luke 9:7–9
✝

Ecclesiastes was written by Qoheleth. On the surface he seems to evoke hopelessness in his words, "All we do in life is vain, useless, soon forgotten." *(Ecclesiastes 1:2)* Wow! Is that right? In some major life areas, the answer is yes. Fortunately, no is also true because life's events and solutions are not just black and white. Sometimes solutions happen within a gray area.

From my own life experiences, some rich things that happened in the various phases remain fresh in my mind. From childhood, loving parents made me sure that I am an OK person. Also, from them, I heard words that convinced me there are right and wrong things to do and say, especially when among people.

My wife's care assures me that our love goes on and that she wishes for other people to care about me, too. Obvious to me from people's remarks, their sincerity, even just their body language, are assurances that they are people loving.

Among my fondest memories is this one: A few weeks ago I was unloading groceries from the grocery cart into my truck. A lady came and loaded them for me, and then without a word she pushed the cart away. I had never seen her before and I have never seen her since. I've enjoyed many kindnesses like this that make me say, "God, you are all loving and you've filled the world with beautiful people just like yourself." God speaks to me through kind acts. Through His helping angels, I hear Him say, "You are fine just the way you are!"

In addition to these warm wonderful ways, though, Qoheleth is quite correct in his cynical remarks that many crucial people and events are forgotten by too many of our greats who could lead the world to peace and happiness. The world suffers as a result. And this is what Qoheleth implies through his critical words.

Our United States of America has for many years been on top of the world and a respected, wealthy world power. But, what people devastatingly forget is before the United States, there were many similar world powers. Like us, they prospered as all their people worked for the well being of one another. God was alive in their midst. Eventually, some became independently wealthy and no longer needed others. They became independent and selfish living richly and powerfully at the top. They forgot God and they crashed. But, then somewhere, humble men and women began again. A great country again grew up, becoming large, comfortable, wealthy, and powerful. Then again, people chose to forget what happened of old and the same pattern was repeated.

You and I know what makes eras great. God blesses all who reach out to the less fortunate. He sends great prophets to lead us. In our own lifetimes He has sent saints to lead us, such as Pope John Paul II and Mother Teresa of Calcutta.

What remains to be seen is this: Will the world's people follow, or will they forget and their great works be in vain? Will our humble beginnings also go by the wayside when we receive God's blessings of wealth? Or will we imitate these prophets from God?

GOD BLESS YOU.

Ephesians 3: 14–21, Luke 12:49–53

✝

Today our gospel does a good job of filling in empty places of Christ's life on Earth and what we can expect as we follow Him into Christianity.

To understand, we need to recall His words from *Luke 4:43* he says, "To other towns, also, I must proclaim the good news of the Kingdom of God. This is why I have been sent." He knows that He will be resented by some wherever He teaches.

In *Luke 12:49* he says, "I have come to set the world on fire, and how I wish it were already blazing!" Fire, of course, purifies, but it also can cause destruction.

John the Baptist said of Him, "He will baptize you with fire…the chaff he will burn in unquenchable flame." *(Luke 3:16)*

Today His words indicate, "I have come, not to bring harmony, but division, division among even the tightest of groups…the family." He also comments, "There is a baptism with which I must be baptized and how great is my anguish until it is accomplished." *(Luke 12:50)*

To follow life as Jesus gives us instructions and example is the only way to fulfillment, but it also leads to unexpected turmoil. He made many loving followers, but some chose to doubt. The doubters eventually crucified Him.

He set the world on fire. Our mission is to follow Him. It calls us to total commitment. During times of a rapidly changing world, peace upon Earth requires very much of us to live 100 percent within God's plans for His people.

We need to hold His values strongly and offer ourselves and movement toward His kingdom, to go forward with His will for the world. This is the fire of our mission.

God calls us to listen to and sympathize with our friends who are hurting from worldly changes. Their hurt feelings are their woes and they need a strong, sympathetic friend.

Always remember that God is in charge! Trust Him to cure these ills. It will all be made OK by our loving God, in His way and time.

GOD BLESS YOU.

CHAPTER 7

UNIQUENESS

Think about the gifts God has given you.
Among them is the gift of total free will
and a unique personality.
The great achievers among us are those who
intently "listen," and then move in the direction
that wisdom takes them.
Each person, being unique, was created to
interpret and then perform individually
according to his or her own talents.

2 Kings 24: 8–17, Matthew 7:21–29

✝

Jesus does not want us to do great things. He just wants us to be available to Him, to be open, and not to feel regret when we need to be His doer.

This means roll up your sleeves and do the work He needs you to do. Be doers, not just talkers.

At the end of His sermon on the mount, He gave a vivid image to emphasize our need to be prepared to create the Kingdom of God on Earth. His words, "Build your house [your life, the center of where and how you live] upon rock. Then the destroying elements cannot nor will not shatter your security." *(Matthew 7:24-29)* Note here that He is saying do not be mediocre at building up the Kingdom. Do all as well as you can. The terms He uses to show our need to build well are, "to be a walker—not a talker."

A "walker" means you face, with confidence, all life with all challenges and situations, have a conscious awareness of the world and people, live wisely, and influence others to have high values.

Pope John Paul II had in his library and read all the books written about the Communist Manifesto. He knew the very weaknesses of communism and was able to handle all its arguments until it fell apart in the country in which it originated. He was a walker.

A talker, on the other hand, tends to put off and ignore the things they are not familiar with. Talkers tend to talk and act foolishly because they are not mentally prepared for the day's tasks. They don't think of anyone beyond themselves and make demeaning, humorous remarks about others' successes.

In regard to self, how often do we get lost in saying much and doing little? Perhaps we should seek to correct this weakness by

---

calling upon God to lead us to be more highly motivated to walk—that is to "do"—what it takes to promote everyone's strengths in their work of building the Kingdom. Do not just talk about what is wrong or trivialize the work of others.

Once we walk as Jesus did, we will grow in wisdom and knowledge about what it means to build upon solid material.

As walkers, let us roll up our sleeves and build upon God's kingdom by living God's story, not just talking about the faults in the church and the world.

Pope Francis today tells us to not get too concerned about correcting the things that are wrong in the church and our nation. Instead, we need to dwell upon and build upon the good things. There is great, great plenty of this to use our wisdom and energy upon!

GOD BLESS YOU.

---

1 Corinthians 3: 18–23/ Luke 5: 1–11

✟

Saint Paul, using his letter to the Corinthians, tells about a force that divides the church of God. It prevents the forming of the one true fold God calls us to. God wants for us to know the world is ours to use, but we must proceed carefully.

We employ creatures, energy, and materials to earn wealth. We likewise form feelings about how we want others to accept us and our ways.

Success causes some to choose to flex their muscles and they may fall victim to the delusion that their power is all they need. These proceed without wisdom, using more than their fair share of God's gifts.

Paul implies that selfish concerns pull individuals away from the unit of the fold and pulling away leads to emptiness. We have seen this happen to some wealthy, famous persons. For them life became a dry desert.

God's gift of wealth in itself does not necessarily make one selfish, but a wealthy person needs to work at continuing to stay active in the organization that binds and understand the benefits that come from sharing.

His message points out that as organized people, the need is to promote unity and to work toward a cause that benefits everyone.

The Gospel of Luke revolves around Jesus' gift of a huge catch of fish to Simon, James, and John. Even though they were tired, they donated their boat to Him so he could teach at a safe distance from the pressing crowd. Most important in this story is not the miraculous catch, but the symbol that by sharing their possessions and following Him, satisfaction grows deep.

We are many different individuals with singular talents. As we withdraw from worldly materials and focus upon God's intended purpose to lead people to Him, we step over walls of factions and form a united movement to accomplish unity. God asks us, through scripture, to analyze the true drives of present-day factions. Then, rather than hurting people, harmoniously work to unite under God's plan and bring a net full of people back to God's church and restore, to an even higher degree, unity to God's one flock.

GOD BLESS YOU.

Philemon 7–20, Luke 17: 20–25
✠

Saint Paul's letter to Philemon is unique and of great interest. It is short, like a good homily. It is read only twice—today and one Sunday in Cycle C. Even more appealing, it treats a hard-to-understand subject. It is the New Testament treatment on slavery.

Philemon was a Christian slaveholder. Onesimus is one of his slaves. He has committed a very serious crime. He ran away! Upon meeting Paul, he was baptized. Paul then sent him back with a letter, hoping, not asking that his master would not kill him (which was the sentence for runaway slaves). The baptized Onesimus is still a slave, but he is now on a kind of equality with his owner.

We do not know if Philemon freed Onesimus. We do presume that he followed Paul's teaching and did not execute him. What we do know is that this letter was shared first with Philemon's family, and was eventually included among the books of the New Testament. Paul counts on Philemon to do the right thing voluntarily, which is the same as God counts on us to do.

In earlier times we were called to fast and abstain under the pain of sin during these liturgical days prior to Christmas and Easter. Today the church asks, instead, to show our love for God by voluntarily following these acts of mortification.

We are invited to do greater acts of love toward the poor and starving. We know that no one person can bring about world peace. No one individual can end worldwide hunger, ensure access to clean drinking water, stop human trafficking, or cure other serious social injustices.

Not being able to do everything, however, does not excuse us from doing what we can. Followers of Jesus need to be the rising yeast of society.

I wish today that you have a very happy, sumptuous Thanksgiving Day and that you remember everything we have. And please do not forget to ask our God to bring some happiness to those who will have no food today!

GOD BLESS YOU.

Joshua 3: 7–10, 13–17; Matthew18: 21–19:1

✝

We hear a beautiful lesson that happened as the Israelites crossed over into the land of plenty.

For the second time on their journey, this God-given miracle of love happened. This was at the end of the rainy season and the Jordan banks were full to the top.

As the Levites, carrying the arc of the covenant, stepped into the river, water walled up on the upper side. On the other side, it flowed on to the sea with dry ground in between.

The ironic thing is that long ago, shortly after the Jews left Egypt, they were at the Jordon shores. Then, many turned their backs because they feared the Philistine giant soldiers who were defenders of the land. They turned their backs and wandered out into the desert, harsh and demanding.

During those forty years, those older men and women who chose this died and were buried there with no one to visit their graves. They were forgotten because they had forgotten God. They failed to have faith in Him who would have stood beside them as their soldiers encountered those giants. They never made it to their promised place of peace and plenty.

Their God-loving leader, Moses, though he was given to see this beautiful land from a mountain top, died and did not get there, either.

Joshua was given this command. He led the Jews in battle, driving out those idolatrous giants.

With God beside them, they moved into the land God had meant for them. They lived peacefully alongside the former people who remained. However, time and comfort wore on. These holy people of God's choice began to return to their ways of idolatry.

God sent them priests through whose hard work many continued to love and honor Him. Many others turned away and lost what God has for all of us.

This is the history of mankind. During desert times we might complain strongly, but during times of plenty many forget God's love and gifts and choose instead those pagan offerings of the world. They find noisy fun that soon dies.

Many pay attention to their priests. These find peace and lasting happiness. They pass on love and laughter and life goes on through them. Some sinners see the truth and return from worldly ways. We all have the freedom to choose to see, to hear, and to seek the delicate path.

Some will fall, forgotten and forlorn. Some will follow their priests into the joys of happy lands. We are not asked to do great things. God asks only that we do small things greatly.

We see happy faces because people go miles to serve. People of honor are there because they have gone to great lengths to help others achieve success.

A number of years ago, I did a research paper on why some athletic coaches get to the top—why they are called to major colleges or to the pros. I was reminded of this earlier this week.

These coaches dedicate themselves to helping each athlete become as good a player as he or she can become. Their win/lose records take care of themselves. These people, like Jesus, are not always liked, but in the end they are honored and followed.

This is what Jesus did. This is what His blessed mother and Father did for Him. This is what brings God's peace and joy. Pay attention to little things and do them with love, extremely well.

GOD BLESS YOU.

Genesis 2:1–19, Matthew 9:1–8

✝

Think about it, friends. The story of Abraham makes a statement about the major challenges of life: He is at one time called by God to leave his secure home and all his relatives and travel to an unknown distant land with only his wife and slaves. He is called to believe that, even in his childless old age, he will father an entire people. His faith is the example of what it means to be chosen by God to become His disciple. Down through all of time Abraham is held up as what faith means.

The first reading shows us the highest point of that faith, the call to let go of one's most cherished possessions to follow God's call.

This reading haunts us, no matter how much we try to explain it. Some scholars say that it was a way to impress upon the chosen people that sacrificing children to pagan gods was wrong. The story ends with God sparing Isaac.

Just what are we to make of this, God's original demand? It calls us to look into our own hearts to see how we reacted when we were called to meet painful demands. Our fears tend to come more from experiences with human beings than our experiences with God. We do believe in a God who is loving and all-knowing, not one who will change His mind.

Beyond this story of love, comes the feeling of peace from the tale that all injustices will one day be corrected. Those who rob our goodness from us will go down in shame, while we, if worthy, will rise to love and laughter. For the times we remained humble and like Jesus before His evil accusers and we said nothing, we will be filled with glory.

Like Simon, who obeyed Jesus and tried fishing one more time after a night of failed fishing, we will rise to success and great rewards far beyond our imagination. Our trials and crosses sometimes deflate us, as it did them. However, as we follow Simon's examples, what God advises, and the example of Jesus as it is flashed before us, we will rise to glory.

The latest reports of the destruction caused by the terrible hurricane Irene tell us that as vicious as it was, the harm done was way less than expected. Many of us did as Jesus and his mother told us to do. We got down on our knees and prayed for God to have mercy upon those living in the storm's path. Among all the devastation and destruction there are some things sent us for relief.

Let me close with these words from our opening prayer, "God, every good thing comes from you. Fill our hearts with love."

GOD BLESS YOU.

2 Thessalonians 2: 1–13, 14–17; Mark 6: 17–29

✠

Growing up the son of a farmer, I found, and still do, some of my heroes among country-loving people and those who work in the outdoors.

A late country singer wrote a song about a six-year-old on a pony ride at the county fair: "Sit tall in the saddle. Hold you head up high. Keep your eyes fixed where the trail meets the sky. Live like you ain't afraid to die. Don't be scared. Just enjoy the ride." *(Chris LeDoux, "The Ride" Capitol Records, 2003)*

Good poets are blessed with special gifts. They teach the messages of Jesus through enjoyable imagery that stays with their readers.

For you and me and all Christians, let's keep our trail meeting the sky at the resurrection. Thus we focus upon a guarantee of a pleasure-filled ride.

Today is dedicated to the beheading of John the Baptist, who along with Jesus and the twelve, lived unafraid to die.

As we meditate upon these deaths, the conclusion comes that seems so senseless. It happened because weak-willed men were manipulated into mistrust and hatred. The instigators were filled with guilt from the Teacher's words. They were afraid, just like many today who never learned that their fear is only a passing thing. They have never learned to approach those they've hurt with the four most powerful words in all human languages: "Will you forgive me?"

In weakness and fear, many who hurt others seek ways to shift blame to those who make them uncomfortable.

I'm sure most have meditated upon people's senseless actions that hurt or raise most fears.

Our great writers, those whose works have become classics, reached their peak of fame because cleverly hidden in their stories was the discovery that senseless decisions would be avoided by applying four humble simple words.

How many unhappy or broken marriages, how many avenging acts would never happen if these four words were spoken? How much peace and joy could reign in the world if the same four words made up the way to where the trail meets the sky?

GOD BLESS YOU.

Ephesians 2: 12–22, Luke12:35–58

✝

Before the gentile Christians in Ephesus became followers of
Jesus, many had worshipped pagan gods whom they were afraid
of because these gods were like jealous and demanding human
beings. In some cases, they were much worse, demanding even
live human male babies to be sacrificed by burning them alive.

The saying, "Eat, drink, and be merry, for tomorrow we may die,"
made sense to many of them. They could not see beyond the
pleasures that come at a single moment. It was not difficult for
Jewish Christians to make gentile Christians feel inferior. After all,
Jewish Christians had worshipped the one true God for centuries,
while the ancestors of the gentile Christians had been worshiping
trees, rivers, and other forces of nature. Paul would not accept
this. He couldn't change the past, but in this letter, he affirms God
had always loved the gentiles and wanted to help them share
equally in the church and divine life.

He knew God's plan needed a long time to work itself out. There
are no second-class members in the church, the family called
together by God. But we are all members of God's household. We
need to be ready for His call. Our generous God will do what no
earthly master would do: wait upon us as if He was our servant.

We do not know when God will call us home. He is saying not to
pat our own backs over our virtues, but to constantly repent
(change) over our past sins and live like Jesus' disciples.

People have always been and will continue to be divided. This will
not change as long as we dwell upon our differences. Peace
comes when we accept the differences, respect individual truths,
and accept all as equals. These are teachings Jesus instituted
through the church and that will lead us to God through justice.

GOD BLESS YOU.

CHAPTER 8

LENT, ADVENT, AND BEYOND

No one can prepare happiness
And salvation for another.
You alone must do it for yourself.
You can find great joy
And excitement in life's challenges
...If you move through each one wisely
And look forward with excitement
To new ones.

Jeremiah 17: 5–10, Luke 16: 19–31

☦

Stop thinking for a few seconds. God is calling. He is saying to empty yourself and listen! Jeremiah tells us this. He, in a very subtle way, is saying to rely upon God and keep that focus.

He also implies that we have been given, through God's holy church, forty special days to work on our listening, to meditate, and to subdue some selfish cravings for foods and for luxuries.

This gospel and this Old Testament reading very subtly give us so much to help us grow and to help us lead others of His people whom He loves with divine love. We hear in them, "The Lord alone sees into your mind and into your heart. Then after death, justice happens! For the just, that is great and eternal joy!"

A very vivid picture is played out here for us. One figure is Lazarus. The other is an unnamed rich man. Our two most precious senses, seeing and hearing, awaken and they give us the freedom to see and hear the beautiful sights and sounds of the world.

The rich man is the symbol of us when we fail to see and hear.

How many times had he stepped over his neighbor at his door? How much food had he thrown away or had overeaten rather than opening his hand to that suffering man? What do you think were the rich man's thoughts? "It is not my problem. Lazarus should get a job to pull himself out of poverty.

God does not detest people with wealth. Many men and women who have been elevated to saints were people of great means including a Holy Roman emperor, Henry II, and Elizabeth of Hungry. These and many others chose to follow their baptismal call to love their neighbor as themselves.

Does God's message come through here for you? Is there a person with some degree of Lazarus in your life? Are there needy people we simply choose to look away from? In the end, will Christ ask, "Why did you not love them as I do? Why did you not love your neighbor?" If these questions do not need to be asked of you, you will have eternity. God's just gift to you will be far more beautiful and joy-filled than any of your greatest days on Earth have been.

Be watchful at how you let yourself feel toward people. He so deeply loves them all. Guard what you look for in others and what you listen to hear. Your just choices will be the causes for joy and beauty for you forever. Look and listen with care. It will likewise cause joy and beauty forever for others God has sent for us to bring home.

GOD BLESS YOU.

Jeremiah 7: 23–28, Luke 11: 114–23

✝

Psalm 95, which we prayed together after the Epistle and before the Gospel says, "If today you hear his voice, harden not your heart." These words seem fair enough and plenty easy to fulfill. And they are because we surely would not do so intentionally. Who would harden his or her heart after hearing God speak?

Upon growing older, however, the depth of what is being asked becomes clearer. God does not speak to me, at least in English, nor does He tap me on the shoulder and say, "Jim, you really should be kinder to your wife." He doesn't send me e-mails reminding me that I haven't been to confession yet this month.

Hearing God's voice is really more a matter of interpreting, for you, where you know God is leading you. We are together, today, in this third week of lent. We are probably having problems with our yoke of Lenten promises and uptight over the fact that Easter is so late, along with the warm weather, which we should have by now. I tap maple trees and make syrup. By now I usually have twenty-five gallons or more of sap. Not a drop has dripped yet.

In reality I do harden my heart as God calls me to remain pleased with what I do have and look ahead in hope. If I am open to hear it, He will help me to remember to soften up a little more.

When I was a young man and came home from fishing with less than a limit, it was not a good fishing day. Today I am happy to get out and if I don't have to clean any fish, I feel the day has been very good!

No matter what the world throws at you, life can still be smilingly beautiful. Keep in mind that God is at your side and His voice is in your heart.

GOD BLESS YOU.

Deuteronomy 30:15–20, Luke 9:22–25

✠

Today we are shown what is different between a person who is filled with wisdom and a person who is just intelligent. Anyone of normal intelligence is capable of accomplishing a high degree of knowledge, success, or honor. Social scientists say that the seemingly smartest people among us uses only a tiny fraction of his or her brain mass.

Intelligence is only one gift we have been given by our loving creator. The other we bestow upon ourselves. People who are wise have acquired wisdom by accepting and working through life's challenges. Challenges come about from a free world and from free people who choose to impose upon the freedom of others so they may gain many earthly possessions.

We achieve wisdom when we simply remember there is a supreme God who bestows justice. Yes, we do need intelligence to work our way through trying circumstances. Then we, too, have a free choice to either hate our aggressor or imitate Jesus on His cross and say, "Father, forgive them. They have no idea of the pain they are passing out. They do not know they are sinning against me and against you."

Moses, in the Gospel, about to die, speaks strongly and wisely, but with deep love and concern. "Keep the Ten Commandments! Love God and Earth and walk in His ways." *(Deuteronomy 30:15)* Summed up, his wise words were, "Obey, honor, and imitate the one who leads you to promised lands."

New Testament wisdom tells us that the way to walk in God's way is to accept the cross. This is not a path we are to choose just once during a time of crisis or pain, but a daily or even hourly choice.

Let's look at ourselves now. Have we lifted our cross today? Do we know what it is? Friends, that is the message of Jesus (and Moses before Him) in the sacred readings. Today's cross may not seem so heavy, but it must be lifted and honored. Might it be a cross of accepting all that comes, even when it's beyond our power to control? Might it be a cross causing us to seem much less than we desire to be, or must we stand up to great difficulty?

We can duck for cover. We can bellyache and act the martyr. Or we can accept today's cross, open our arms, and lift it high. Then you have made it a holy moment by your free choice.

Moses had been wandering in the desert for forty years when he challenged his people to "hold fast." Jesus was predicting suffering and death when He said, "Take up your cross." You will know deserts and suffering, perhaps even today. Choose what comes. Make today a walk in the way of the Lord, a path that leads to eternal life. Lent calls us to small sacrifices and love for it all, then beauty comes to behold.

GOD BLESS YOU.

Zephaniah 3:14–18, Philippians 4:4–7, Luke 3: 10–18

✞

The previous two chapters of Zephaniah's book cry a warning that disaster is about to happen to God's chosen people because they, along with their leaders, have turned away from God and are ignoring their poor.

This particular reading is appropriately chosen for the third Sunday of Advent. This is Rejoice (Gaudete) Sunday. It sings to the captive Israelites that their captivity in Babylon is ended. God is saying, through Zephaniah, to stop bemoaning and rejoice because "You are being released and are free to return to the land of your ancestors." One hundred years ago they had become captives and now all they knew about their homeland was from stories about what it was like in the time of their exile.

The prophet is telling these Jewish people that their loving God has forgiven the sins of their ancestors and that He is a loving and forgiving God. Their sins have been forgiven and forgotten. God is now restoring them to the promised land and they will find happiness and peace by going home. "Go home and reunite with your loving God."

Rejoice Sunday comes nine days before the birthday of our Redeemer.

Here the Zephaniah story ties up with Luke's Gospel in which John the Baptist comes on the scene to prepare the people to meet Jesus. He makes the path straight for his cousin, who comes teaching, and then all flesh sees the salvation of God.

Jesus came to teach at John's death. The book of Zephaniah begins with defeat and exile, and ends with that prophet singing about release from sin, their freedom to go home, and a promise of the care of their loving God. This Gospel story shows John on the scene, strongly scolding the Jews for their sins. "You brood of

----

vipers are guilty of God's coming wrath. Produce good fruit as evidence of your repentance. Even now an axe lies at the root of the trees. Every tree that does not produce good fruit will be cut down and thrown into the fire." *(Luke 3:10-18)*

Many sinners came to him there and asked what to do. His answer was that they must first of all share what they own with the poor. Among those who came for forgiveness were the highly hated tax collectors who had overcharged the poor and kept the excess money. Soldiers came. Their sins were abuse of the poor, false accusations, and extortion. And at John's strong and honest words, they repented and were rejoicing.

This, my friends, is the story to us during these four weeks of Advent. As we pass through this season, day by day, and hear God's story of love and forgiveness and the true joy that comes to us who hear, know that this same God exists today! He is right beside us offering us this same love, forgiveness, and joy. It tells us that this all comes to us in the same amount that we give it away, especially to those in need.

GOD BLESS YOU.

Isaiah 40:25–31, Matthew 11:28–30

✟

"I am meek and humble of heart!" Forever, before time existed, an inconceivable knowledge, a power, a love like no-one knows existed. They existed and still exist in a state away beyond imagination. At home, in eternity, we will then see the face of God.

On Earth, in heaven, and perhaps, even in hell this spirit exists. These lines from Matthew tell us that "He" is that energy that happened and from which all happens.

Today, those words of Isaiah's tell us simply what it means to live as much of God's ways as is possible for humans. The meek and the humble fit right into the very being of God. His presence in people strengthens the faint of heart, revives the weary, and brings rejoicing.

There is a line here worth repeating over and over and over again. It is the last line from Isaiah: "They that 'hope' in the Lord will renew their strength; they will run and not grow tired, walk and not grow faint," a fitting thought for our advent journey.

Psalm 103:2 was read today and it is a brilliant description of God. "Lest we forget, God is, above all, merciful and gracious, and abounding in kindness."

Friends, who besides God forgives, heals, redeems, and crowns with compassion, goodness, peace, and love and still gives total freedom for us to make choices? That is who God really is.

Listen again to the one, true, total perfect line from God, Jesus of Nazareth, son of humankind, son of God: "Come to me, all you who are burdened, and I will give you rest. Take my yoke upon you, and learn from me. For I am meek and humble and you will find rest for yourselves. For my yoke is easy, and my burden light." *(Matthew 11:28-30)* Jesus fully reveals God here in these

----

words and invites us to see intimately into God. "Come follow me."
He keeps calling, and His way is the sure path to God.

So when we become in need of a journey into peace, where do
our choices lie? We may dream of what we should have said or
done in a depressive situation. We also may accept the light
weight of the cross and do what Jesus would do. Then we will
have peace and joy and experience God, who is all, who is beside
us in the states of love, peace, and forgiveness. It takes no more
energy to discipline our choice to accept Him than it does to
choose anger.

And God is far sweeter to have.

GOD BLESS YOU.

Isaiah 26:1–6, Matthew 7:21,24–27

✝

In these early days of advent we hear of Yahweh's dream for His people, Israel. Isaiah says that Yahweh dreams of us, His beloved children living on His mountaintop and being in His home! He describes God's home as one of justice, peace, unity, and no discrimination, where all His beloved are one in mind. He offers forgiveness, reconciliation, and trust as a state of being. We are destined and desired by God to live love.

However, as with any parent, God will not "make" the dream a reality. It is up to us to grow into the dream. God invites, loves, and trusts us to actively live His dream. He desires! He yearns, but the final choice is ours.

Isaiah assures us God will be with us, encouraging us if we trust Him.

In Matthew's Gospel Jesus says, "Only the one who does the will of my Father will enter the kingdom of Heaven."

How are we to know the "what" and "how" of it?

Jesus is the known facility for us to see God's desire, God's dream. He is the way and the light. He is the struggle for justice, peace, and joy. He works with us through dishonesty, lies, deceit, through anger, violence, jealousy. Jesus is with us as we live into God's desire.

Advent is referred to as the time of waiting for justice, peace, and order and for healing, death, and the Kingdom.

We wait in vain if we are not active. "Your kingdom come. Your will be done." Who is to usher us into the Kingdom? God is waiting for us to act out His holy will. . . We wait!

GOD BLESS YOU.

Isaiah 26:1–6, Matthew 7:21, 24–27

✝

Let me paraphrase Matthew's line so packed with wisdom. This puts it into simple words and belts out his meaning. "A wise man builds his house on rock, then, even when powerful destructive forces pound it, it will stand sturdy to the very end of its required use to its builder. At that time it will have served the builder with comforts and peace while his purpose on earth he gets done."

We know that the item, this house, stands for us, and the way we hold up under life's stresses. It is how and where we build our relationship with God. That solid rock is the church, along with the Bible. The sand foundation beneath the house that falls is temporary worldly attractions. Whichever we choose is our own decision.

The outside forces that pummel our house come from all manner of elements: stress, temptations, sin, internal and external conflicts, etc. They wear us down, sometimes to the point that it seems our house will tumble and we see no way we can stop it. We may even feel that God has left us to the world.

One of God's great gifts is to turn back to His loving promises at this time of Advent. Through observance we move in our way back. We find Him in our possessions. Advent replays His birth here on Earth. As a baby, He came. He grew up. He walked on the ground of our Earth among our Christian ancestors. He gave His life in body on the cross to open heaven. Knowing and feeling Him present gives the grace to rebuild our relations with Him upon the solid foundation of His words and the example He set for us. Here we will stand up to even the most evil blows.

Advent is His hand of love reaching to give us strength to live in peace and justice. It is, again, our time to anticipate His coming and to grow in our journey to heaven.

Christmas tells the story. Just as he gives, we give. We give to one another and become happy when someone is delighted with our gift. This is one small experience here on Earth of the beautiful joy of eternity in heaven. Our gifts say I love you. God's gifts say I love you, regardless of your imperfections.

As God flaunts His love of us, let's never forget the most powerful gift we can give Him is prayer. He answers and through prayers for others, we touch Jesus and seek meaning in His words.

This advent let us dwell on this. No matter what our situation, we can always give because God hears our prayers and we can hear His answers when we are quiet and at peace.

God's wisdom to us in all this is you are not strangers and aliens. You are fellow citizens of the saints and members of the household of God. You form a building that rises on the rock—the foundations of the apostles and the prophets with Jesus as the cornerstone. Through Him the whole structure is put together and takes shape as a holy temple in the Lord. In Him you are built into this temple to become a dwelling place for God in the Spirit.

St. Eustache
Church, Paris

2nd week of Advent
2013

Acts 11:21–26,13:1–3; Matthew 5:20

✝

We read and hear works written by the Apostles daily. There is no doubt about how devout and sincere their love for Jesus was. Likewise, they took what he taught absolutely seriously. Today, Saint Paul and Matthew pass on, to us, His lesson on nonviolence and reconciliation.

Jesus used the fifth commandment to make His point. "You shall not kill; whoever kills will be liable to judgment. But I say to you, whoever is angry with his brother will be liable to judgment."

To truly understand these phrases, we have to understand that Jesus is really playing with our minds to make His point.

Does His use of the word judgment mean our final judgment at the end of the world? The answer is no! In those ancient times, judgment meant by the Sanhedrin, equivalent to our Supreme Court. If we kill someone, we were and are judged by our fellow humans. On the other hand, being angry at someone is not cause to go before human court. He, Himself, will justly be our judge. In the same vein He says, "Whoever says to another, 'you foul' will be liable to the fiery Gehenna." Now Gehenna was a former pagan sight outside of Jerusalem used as a garbage dump. Today it is synonymous with this idea.

So, what is all this about? Is He saying anger is a sin? Again, the answer is no! Upon being abused or defamed, it is human nature to get mad. It becomes a sin only when we continue to nurse it and allow it to become a part of our lives. Mounting anger will eventually lead one to defamation of another's good name, and it can even lead to murder.

The intent Jesus wants to instill in us is for us to surpass what human's law cannot touch. His challenge is for us to manage our anger. Used properly, it will lead to growth into higher more noble

---

heights. Then it becomes a blessing. Dwell not upon the pain caused by another, but, rather upon climbing above the smallness of hurting the other in return.

This requires prayerful attention to our emotional life. The Holy Spirit can heal the darkest stuff if we expose it to the light of prayer.

If your hostility gets really aggressive, read Jesus' teachings on nonviolence and love of enemies at the end of Matthew's fifth chapter.

GOD BLESS YOU.

Acts 1: 15–17, 20–26; John 15: 9–17

✝

In days of old, this day would have been a holy day of obligation. Though we make it holy by the things we do, going to Mass is not an obligation because, as you know, our hierarchy moved the day to honor Jesus' Ascension to the next Sunday.

On this day, Jesus left His twelve Apostles and they then had to discover reality for themselves. No longer is He with them to take the burden off their shoulders. Now they have complete charge in making their own choices. T

hey make mistakes and wisdom is gained. So what does this say to us? Jesus explains here that we, like His apostles, also must make choices. At times we choose wrong, but we become wiser after correcting our mistakes.

Throughout human history parents have had to choose. How much freedom should they give their children? How many restrictions should they place on their children to live by? Then with charity, where do we draw the line on giving? Too much prevents receivers from growing strong in soul and mind. Good character and holiness happen from within, not from the outside.

No one can do this for anyone else. Everyone must fail or succeed on His own. This is a privilege. Growth happens when we struggle to accept God's graces to get there. Only when we own the lessons we learn are they truly ours.

That is exactly what Jesus gave to His friends. Only when He ascended, leaving the disciples to go it alone to make mistakes and to suffer, did the grace of knowledge and truth take deep root in their minds and souls. No longer could they fall back on Jesus. He was gone. They could turn to the Holy Spirit for the wisdom and courage to grow, but the journey was theirs to walk. Jesus' departure did them a favor.

"You will be my witness" were the last words to them as he was lifted up before their eyes and disappeared. These men and women learned well from Him. They became witnesses, and they became saints. We are to do the same thing. We are witnesses wherever God plants us. God is with us in the Holy Spirit. Now it is our turn to think and act on our own. The Kingdom of God is depending on you and me.

GOD BLESS YOU.

Acts 13:13–25, John 13:16

✝

Acts tells us tales and gives us a glimpse into the work of the greatest missionaries the church has ever known. In today's first reading, Paul faces a situation similar in a way to one we face in our daily lives. It is the opportunity to take the stage and the opportunity to serve the Lord.

We are offered the same opportunity every day. Ours, though, is not as big and glorious as His. He was asked to go up before the crowd in the synagogue. This would compare to our addressing a full assembly in the Cathedral. Our task, like His, is just as important to accept.

How often do we witness people talking negatively about common things in everyday life such as about others' faults? Each of these situations is, for us, an opening to share our Catholic faith through God's love and peace with those around us.

But what do I, as a mere parishioner, have to offer my brothers and sisters when they give me those chances? Certainly, I don't have the expertise of Saint Paul or of my pastor. I haven't had a good lesson focusing upon things of this world in order to increase my giving to Jesus.

But my experiences with Lent, have shown me that, yes, I can refuse myself these things. From here I can discipline myself to not only refuse to gossip, but also to speak positively about the people and situations that pass by me in life. Each of these situations is a perfect offering to use the lessons offered to me by the Holy Spirit that were spoken into my heart. Here is a beautiful chance to take what we've gathered in prayer, fasting, and self-denials and turn them into service to others around us.

God spends a lot of time on the topic of mercy, especially during Lent. Could I, likewise, offer mercy to someone who is suffering

---

from stress or fatigue instead of gossiping about his or her mistakes? Wouldn't it be more correct of me to show the person mercy, give her or him the benefit of the doubt, or at least change the subject?

But Paul doesn't stop at accepting the challenge to speak when offered. He invites others to know Jesus as he does. We have just witnessed the joy of those receiving baptism at the Easter Vigil—the joy of those celebrating their first communion with God in the Holy Catholic Church. It is truly something to share the peace that comes into the lives of these men and women.

Let us invite them to enjoy our faith. Let's accept their small invitation to share God's love with them. For ten or more years, I worked in the RCIA program, and even today those people come to me with thank yous and warm smiles. These simple yet profound choices can make us missionaries like Paul, and perhaps even the saints!

GOD BLESS YOU.

Acts 15:7–21, John 15:9–11

✝

One of the most remarkable things Jesus said to his Apostles and says to us is, "As the Father loves me, so I love you." It is really hard to imagine how much the Father loves Jesus because it is a love that is extraordinary. Jesus says that He loves us just as much as God loves him. He does, though, love you and me that much. Imagine it! He loves me—as much as the Father loves him.

He asks me to *remain* in His love. It is so very difficult to even get myself there. Then how can I keep myself there? Saint Augustine tells us that we were made to make our home in that love, and our hearts just are not at peace until they rest there.

Reflecting upon what makes my heart restless, I come up with things offered by the world: temptations, self-pity, anxieties, fears, and just things. These call to me, strongly, to make my home among them.

It comes down to becoming aware of what drags me on to keep grasping for things that fail to satisfy me, or to grasp for more and more things that cause me to elude freedom and peace.

Becoming aware of these, I can then see to make choices that satisfy. I can let go of feelings like anger and stress. Once I do that, my entire perspective will change. I will see clearly that these habits disrupt good health, happy relationships, and freedom.

Jesus says He loves us with everlasting love. I am now faced with the opportunity to welcome this love and become alive in it. Once that happens I will no longer cling to what makes me unhappy and leaves me empty. I will be in His love. I will be centered in peace I can feel. I will feel what being loved allows me to do. I will no longer be afraid to express my love, and I will be capable of compassion and mercy.

That is what I hope you will ask for today: To desire this grace, or even just want the desire for it.

Let me end with a prayer: I hope to make my home in your love for me, dear Jesus. I long to remain in your love, today, and then I will give myself to loving others as you love me.

GOD BLESS YOU.

Exodus 3: 13–20, Matthew 11:28–30

✝

Saint Matthew gives us a beautiful overview today of the way Jesus tells the Israelites and us who need to be reminded often about "why" God has put his commandments before us. Following them provides that happy, stress-free life. "My yoke, my requests are light and peace filled to you who accept them." To get the entire picture, we need to look at the yoke of the Pharisees. About them, Jesus says, "They are burdens placed on the shoulders of the people; burdens too heavy to carry."

The Jews had 613 laws covering everything from Sabbath rest to washing dishes. People became ritually unclean if they touched a corpse or ate with Gentiles. And there were many other ways to become unclean. No matter how hard folks tried, they fell short and the burden of guilt was heavy for them because of the ever-growing interpretations of those laws.

In contrast, Jesus' yoke is simple: "Love God, and love your neighbor as yourself." He knows that at times we will fail, but his mercy covers our guilty feelings. He, Himself, paid for our weakness by dying on the cross.

It is because of our failures and/or those of others that stress is induced. Stress is our reminder to slow down from life and shoulder God's light and peace-building burden: "Come to me and I will give you rest."

At hand for us He offers personal prayers, along with those that come to us when we participate in Mass. As we settle down and meditate upon the prayers recited by our priests, these settle into our hearts like a warm soothing bath or like having coffee with friends, or like working in our gardens.

He encourages us even further: "Learn from me. I am meek…and my heart is humble." He shows us the way away from power-

---

driven, arrogant people. He says that we can be yoked to 613 laws of the Old Testament or take on "His" yoke, which is easy and light.

If we come to God, meek and humble, we will realize His holy love, and life turns peaceful. As His children, we are called to be obedient. And, my dear friends, Jesus led the way for us. If we take any yoke other than the one God places on us, we are bearing unnecessary burdens. It is our choice!

GOD BLESS YOU.

Acts 2, 14: 22–33, 1Peter 1:17–21, Luke 24: 13–35

☩

What a very descriptive way to say it: "Were not our hearts burning within us while He spoke to us on the way and opened the scriptures to us?"

During their three years together, everything in the life of the disciples changed. Their old lives vanished. Just who were they before they met Jesus and answered His call? Their families, at first, begged them to stop the foolishness and come home. Who will support the children? After years, however, the whole family became active members and followers of Jesus and His mission.

In the company of Jesus they knew who they were. But He was torn from them, brought to trial before those fickle men who had formerly loved Him. He was tortured and crucified as an enemy, this man of healing power and one who preached forgiveness. Fear and confusion filled them. All but a few ran away.

To be abandoned is piercing pain. Jesus was left alone amid the brutal people with deep loneliness, but he did not abandon them. Easter Sunday afternoon, two disciples shared their troubles with a stranger. They were struggling to make sense of the horror. The stranger traced the events leading to the death of their beloved companion all the way back to Moses! His words settled them, but it was the breaking of the bread that opened their eyes.

As we search the words and signs for who we are, we can get discouraged if we don't find something familiar. But, our great Pope Francis helps us believe the death and resurrection of Christ is the heart of the Gospel. Here we discover that we are not alone on the road. This joy gave Peter the courage to speak to the Jews about the man their leaders killed, and who rose from the dead, who, when found, brings joy we cannot keep to ourselves.

GOD BLESS YOU.

Colossians3:12–17, Luke 6:27–38

✝

These readings really set you back on your heels because they tell us—not hint—to "love as Jesus loved." To love and not to count the cost. To love as God loves us. This is way above what I can fathom.

Thinking about these readings, I ask whether these commands accommodate our love for precious life? Or my prideful drive to protect my loved ones who trust me to keep them safe? These human drives are true drives of a normal being whose pride dictates a desire to "come out fighting." See here how over and over all of God's commands say we need to be peaceful and Him. He will see that justice wins out! And this is what critics of Christianity dwell on because if we fail to fight, we will be overrun, our possessions taken, and we will be smeared into the dirt. Not a pretty picture, and it seems so true.

How do we defend acceptance and peace against what the world has always thought of as reality? The answer lies hidden in that little lettered abbreviated question, WWJD?

We all "know" what Jesus did two thousand years ago. He went silently before his angry Jewish people, before Pontius Pilot, and before Annas. He allowed all their hatred to be played out upon Him and He died. He silently accepted skin-tearing lashes, let them spit in His face, staggered beneath the heavy cross up Calvary, let His feet be nailed to the upright, His hands to the crosspieces, then all this was raised up with Him hanging in this horrible picture several hours until He mercifully died.

Before dying, He said, "Father, please forgive them." *(Luke 23:34)* And this was not the end - It was the beginning! The fresh beginning to the existence of peace on Earth! Saint Paul and Saint Matthew are telling us if we were strong enough to silently accept the worst that anyone can ever hand out, we would lead the world

----

to God's will. We *can* have heaven on Earth, because that is the way it *is* in heaven. All of us are filled with deep love and beautiful peace, but what happens to our faculties when danger or disorder strike? Being human we become fearful. Fear leads us to break down and we come out fighting mad.

But God is very direct to us today. Very plainly, He says to do what Jesus would do! He tells us, over and over, how our saints found peace among all the messes. Among them was one true person, the Blessed Virgin Mary. Imagine *her*! She watched her son being crucified! She stood beside Him hanging lifeless on the cross! She hugged his broken body on her lap before they buried it, and we are told she never once became angry at God. She loved deeply, she sorrowfully accepted, she was at peace through it all.

From all this comes His church. Under the guidance of Saint Peter and the great line of Popes, under the knowledge that our pope and bishops have the keys to heaven, our priests will after our repentance, forgive our sins. That this will forever withstand any attacks that hell will ever throw against us. Try as they may to destroy us, what God has created will live strong in peace and will bring us home.

Our loving God is always telling us to, "Do it the way my Son did it, in love, and my Kingdom is yours on Earth and in heaven."

GOD BLESS YOU.

Mary—given to us when we left Our Lady of the Snows in Bigfork—stands out front in the beautiful garden of flowers at our lake place; near our former home.